THE BOOK
OF BOATS

THE BOOK
OF BOATS

Edited by

WILLIAM and JOHN
ATKIN

Assisted by
BILL W. ATKIN
DORCAS ATKIN and
SHIRLEY KRAMER

International Marine Publishing Company
Camden, Maine

To
WILLIAM ATKIN

1882 — 1962

Contents
Part One

Part Two

Preface to the New Edition

I appreciate Roger Taylor and the International Marine Publishing Company putting the two *Books of Boats* together and making them available again. Some thirty years ago my late father and I gathered this material and published The *First* and *Second Book of Boats* — a collection of work relating to wholesome power and sailing yachts.

It is interesting, and rather amazing, that considerable enthusiasm continues to exist for traditional designs — it has been said that "good design cannot be outdated" — despite the tremendous transition the yachting field has experienced since the end of the Second World War and the introduction of fiberglass reinforced plastics. There is an entire generation of yachtsmen who have no concept or appreciation of the wonders, simplicity, and ease of handling of traditional yachts. They have the mistaken impression that all sailing yachts are quick, tender, unnecessarily complicated and decidedly uncomfortable. And all around them are powerboats that are very often over-powered and equally complex! Despite this, there is every indication that interest in wholesome yachts will continue to grow and prosper.

My father and I had thoughts of working three or four days a week, when the War ended, to muck about in our own *We're Here* on days off. But growing high taxes, the pressure of work, and ultimately inflation brought these thoughts to an end! We both kept very busy — one way or another — satisfying the desires of clients. Billy Atkin departed on his voyage to Valhalla in August, 1962, after spending a lifetime engaged in designing and writing about little ships. Few folks, indeed, are rewarded by such a long association with "Shipmates" the world over — all sharing a common interest related to the little ships he loved so well. I continue to keep my hand in the development of small power and sailing yachts — "individualized designs for unregimented yachtsmen" — but my main activity involves the pre-purchase surveying of various yachts. While this activity isn't as much fun as designing, it is continually enlightening and thus a most rewarding endeavor.

The original *First* and *Second Book of Boats* contained advertising pages, and without these we could not have produced the books. Thus it seems appropriate to mention the following firms who advertised in the initial publications and who are very much in evidence today:

M. L. Condon Lumber Co.
G.M. Diesels
Champion Spark Plugs
W. W. Norton Publishing Co.
International Paint Co.
American Brass
Pigeon Hollow Spar
Louis J. Larsen & Sons
John E. Hand & Sons

Merriman Bros.
Universal Engine Company
H. B. Fred Kuhls
Columbian Bronze Corp.
The Lincoln Electric Co.
Lloyd's Register
Buffalo Fire Appliance Co.
Thomas Gillmer
William Garden

We wrote in the original books, "somehow the advertising pages are as much a part of this pastime of yachting and boating as the pages of editorial material. And this is particularly true if the advertisers are of high caliber, and if not of high caliber we do not believe they should be accepted as Shipmates." I feel I would be remiss not to include these Shipmates who supported our efforts in the past and remain firms of "high caliber."

Billy Atkin designed *Buddy II*, a V bottom "auto-boat," in 1906; this was his first design. Seventy years have now slipped to leeward, the design number is now 861 — the majority of these were drawn by Billy, until I joined him after the War in 1946 — and most of these were done by the two of us without benefit of outside help.

The *First Book of Boats* was dedicated to yacht designer William P. Stephens (1855-1946), the *Second Book* to yachtsman Stephen D. Baker (1868-1944). It is perhaps fitting on this 70th anniversary of Billy's start that the combined *Book of Boats* be dedicated to William Atkin (1882-1962), who was responsible for putting wholesome "little ships" on paper, so that those designs could grow to realities virtually the world over. In his later years Billy wrote, "time may always catch up, Shipmates, but I have had a great deal of fun eluding it." And that he did.

John Atkin
Noroton, Connecticut
June, 1976

THE BOOK
OF BOATS

Part One

Foreword

THE material presented in the pages of this, THE FIRST BOOK OF BOATS, has been selected only after very careful consideration and its editing and preparation have required many months of time. Some of it is old; so old, that to the younger generation of cruising men it will be new. Some of it, I suppose I might say, is middle-aged and, despite this, is as timely today as it was when written a generation ago. Much of it is new and refreshing because it refers to the work of a number of yacht designers and writers who are new to the pastime of yachting as it concerns small boats today.

THE FIRST BOOK OF BOATS does not aspire to be a digest of articles and plans that have been published in books and magazines. At best, digests are misleading because he who does the digesting is likely to have an axe to grind, a whim to satisfy, or an enemy to break. And if your digest man happens to be the opinionated sort, like several I know, then the digest will be quite without value of any kind. No, Shipmates, this little book is not a yachting digest.

And while it is a book in form, THE FIRST BOOK OF BOATS is Volume 1 of a quarterly periodical. Each volume is complete in itself; but each is a component of the series for the year. And so when December comes will come THE SECOND BOOK OF BOATS; and with March the THIRD BOOK and so on down the years to come. I feel it will be a happy prospect for those genuine people who find fun and contentment in the joy there is in useful little yachts and boats.

Perhaps in the bewilderments of a modern world where almost everything is highly appraised because of its hugh size, its gaudy expanse of chromium plate, its marvelous complication, its industrial stream-lining, its tremendous popularity, and the noisy bally-hooing accompanying it all, the wholesome, plain and genuine character of THE BOOK OF BOATS series will fill a place in the cabin book shelves which have for many years been empty.

It is fitting, I feel, that I should include in these pages an appreciation of five excellent American magazines. For the best part of fifty years these have been sincerely edited and consistantly published in the interests of all those folks who find recreation and entertainment in the use and contemplation of all those things that have to do with boats, sails, engines, and with the rivers, the lakes, and the sea. I have contributed to four of these, and have been editor of one. These magazines will be MOTOR BOATING, RUDDER, PACIFIC MOTOR BOAT, MOTOR BOAT, and YACHTING. My affection for these may be measured by the order in which I have written them, and I feel I am not far at sea if I also feel that the aid they have given the boat and engine industry and the desire they have developed for practical, wholesome, useful, and sensible sailing boats and power boats will remain in the same sequence. The time I spend in reading these magazines is spent to excellent advantage and they pile up in our office, drafting room and dwelling and even into my son John's Dinghy Shed because I dislike to throw any one of them away. And I sincerely hope, Shipmates, you take the advice of an old hand and read all five as I do. I often wonder where the pastime and industry would be were it not for the valuable assistance the boating magazines have given these.

I have always been a practical man with a gift for working with my own hands—and also with my own head—and as the years have rolled past they have given to me first hand experience with the tools, materials, and processes required for building boats of all kinds; boats that are shipshape despite their dimensions, and wholly adaptable for the service they are designed to perform. And in the matter of all this one would be stupid not to have learned a great deal about construction and the materials to avoid when building. For instance, I would not, for my own use, use plywoods of any kind for the outside parts of a boat and I should use this material very sparingly for inside work. It seems silly to me to boil wood; slice thin layers from it; press these together with heat and glue; and then market it in big sheets that are difficult and expensive to handle. Wouldn't it be better to use the wood without the expensive processing which turns it into plywood? At any rate, I think so. There is also this matter of rot proofing and the arresting of dry rot. The fault of one of these extensively advertised products is that the cure is worse than the disease because the cure-all corrodes any metal it touches, and this to an alarming degree.

Here are instances indicating the kind of things that will not be advertised in the BOOK OF BOATS series. Somehow I am sure this is a policy that is in the interest of better materials for things afloat. I do not depreciate the advantage which new products have brought into the world of boats, but I am old enough to know that everything advertised has not, one might say, the quality of cloth of gold. It is unfortunate for the purchaser that this is so. I am a believer in progress by evolution rather than by revolution, and evolution is, by its very nature, a slow and tedious process; I fear too tedious for hasty minded young engineers and business men all set to hurry the future into today.

This being the machine age and the heyday of quantity production, it is inevitable that boats are beginning to look so much alike. This from an aesthetic standpoint, is little short of tragedy. I often wonder where this will lead us. Fortunately there will always be unregimented yachtsmen whose wants cannot be filled with duplications, and to these the following letter will have special significance:

* * *

THIRTY FOOT ATKIN CUTTER; SOME WHAT
Marie-Princess; SOME WHAT *Ben Bow.*

A drawing by
William Law,
Lt. Col. U. S. Army

4

Something to remember

James S. Pitkin

I KNOW a yachtsman who married a pretty widow. She owned an inland farm on the crest of a Connecticut hill. The view was cycloramic. He said that you could see for miles on every point of the compass. But you couldn't see salt water. As a matter of fact, he hadn't seen salt water for several summers and didn't know when, if ever, he would see it again.

But he told me that sometimes when he was pitching hay on the upland pasture, and the fluffy cumulous clouds were drifting southward across the blue, he would lean on his pitchfork and estimate the force of the breeze. And presently he would be cruising again, with all sail set and lee rail under, making a fast run down the Sound and through Plum Gut to Greenport, or through the Race to Block Island! He saw it so distinctly that it was like a motion-picture in full color. And he would stand there, completely oblivious of his surroundings, for half an hour at a time.

That's the way it is with yachtsmen. They never forget. They have memories that afford them a means of escape. Memories of another way of life, in which competition is replaced by cooperation. Where every man stands ready to give his all, if need be, to rescue a fellow seaman. For it's a grand, unselfish world, this realm of the sea, based on noble tradition and heroic precedent.

And thus it is that, when you put to sea in your own boat, you become a different and, for the time being at least, a better man. Instead of competing with other men, you are contending with the wind and the waves. The familiar profit motive is replaced by an instinct for self-preservation, strangely superseded by a desire to assist others; which is a wholesome change, not devoid of pleasurable excitement.

And then again, when you sit at the helm of your little ship on a clear night, and gaze at the countless stars overhead, and realize that you are quite alone on a wide, wide sea, it is apt to occur to you that in the general scheme of things you are merely an insignificant speck on the surface of the ocean; and are not nearly so important nor so self-sufficient as you thought you were. Which is an exceedingly wholesome thought, and one that may effect a permanent change in your deportment that will be greatly appreciated by your friends.

Therefore, I advise you most earnestly to obtain a boat—preferably of Atkin design. But I must warn you against marrying a girl who owns a farm, or one who loves the ocean when it's rough, or one who adores a fog, because they, one and all, lack the intuitive seagoing sense that a seaworthy wife should have. And if you marry one of them you will find yourself on an inland farm, or an inland lake, or in a mountain camp, watching the clouds sail southward to the sea.

'Little' Diablesse

Frederic A. Fenger

FOR an ex-schooner man of gaff-headed days who thought he would never be content in any craft under fifty feet on deck, the much smaller and far more modern thirty-eight foot *Diablesse* has proven the worth of the "little ship". And while it seems rather out of place for a designer to extol his own wares, some general comments on this type, after six seasons of cruising—ex-war years—may be in order.

First intended for a New York client, for whom a sister-ship was built, there were no hampering "owner restrictions" beyond those of size and berthing, so that absolute freedom—that mental elbow-room which gives life to most top-ranking craft—largely may be credited for the satisfaction she has given.

Much has been written on the planning of small auxiliaries, yet the art of creating comfort and the impression of spaciousness hardly has been touched upon. Elimination of side seats and a slight lowering of the bridge deck, not only widens one's standing room but gives it more apparent depth which adds to the feeling of security in a seemingly enlarged cockpit, while restful angles in the "buggy seats" on either side of the wheel box take most of the chore out of long enforced tricks at the helm. Relatively wide waterways invite one to walk the decks that somehow have stretched her out to a forty-two footer. It is surprising how substantial life lines, well stanchioned, expand one's working area by half. Inboard, almost knee-high house sides moor one's under-pinning in a seaway—a strong argument against the Semitic curves of the "streamlined" over-crowned hummocks which are an abomination to the eye and make for "giddy footing", as Shakespeare had it.

The cramping of hatches, skylights and companionways only tend to emphasize the smallness of one's craft, whereas if these openings are held to comfortable proportions or even accentuated in size, they suggest the ship rather than the "tabloid" cruiser.

An ample companionway, then, whose wide ladder is shortened a step due to the lowered bridge deck, and laid out with deep treads and broad throws, takes one below with no hint of being "cabin'd, cribb'd,

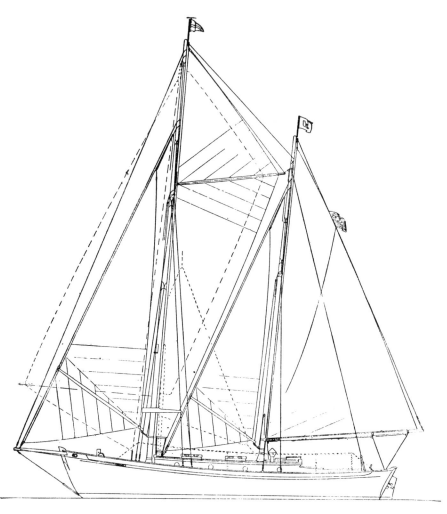

'Little' Diablesse IS RIGGED AS A "WISH BONE" KETCH. DESPITE HER DIS-
PUTED SAIL PLAN, WHICH IS MODEST WHEN COMPARED TO THE YACHT'S
DISPLACEMENT, *'Little' Diablesse,* IS A VERY SMART AND CLOSE WINDED
VESSEL. THE SMALL UNITS COMPRISING THE SAIL PLAN MAY BE EASILY
HANDLED WHEN SAILING ALONE. THE WELL SPACED MASTS ARE OF
INTEREST.

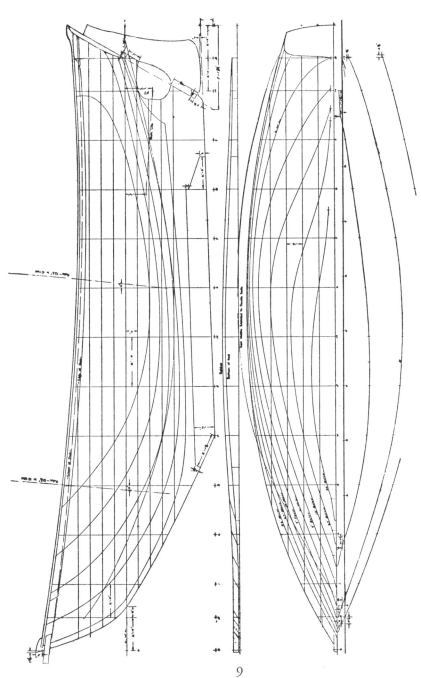

THE LINES SHOW A BEAUTIFULLY BALANCED HULL OF WHOLESOME DISPLACEMENT AND POWER. NOTICE THE GREATEST DRAFT IS AT THE FORWARD END OF THE KEEL AND TYPICAL OF THE DHOWS OF THE EASTERN MEDITERRANEAN SEA.

9

confined." Again Will Shakespeare who must have been something of a small boatman himself, on the narrow seas about him. Under six feet three inches of clear headroom the cabin sole spreads four feet between the transoms so that one may have a wide-topped table with end-drawers, well secured for support in a seaway. All this because of generous freeboard and somewhat at the expense of sleek "yachtiness", but a sturdy vessel looks all the better for such proportioning.

A mirror, secured at a proper working angle in the forward end of the stateroom will reflect an elongating vista that expands one's view as though the bulkhead had receded by a berth's length.

Gadgets, on the other hand, "clever stows", protruding book shelves, and other devices to relieve one's ordinary stowage spaces, should be courted with deliberation and then unobtrusively placed, if at

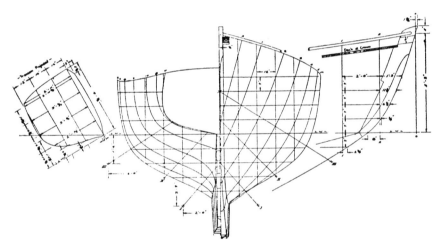

THE BODY PLAN OF '*Little*' *Diablesse* SHOWS A NICE BALANCE BETWEEN THE FORWARD AND AFTER SECTIONS, ABOVE AS WELL AS BELOW THE LOAD WATER LINE. THE FIRMNESS OF THE BILGES SPELL STABILITY AND THE FLARE OF THE TOPSIDES DRYNESS.

all, lest they clutter and thus defeat the impression of spaciousness. One should attain the feeling of coziness without turning one's cabin into a marine hock shop.

The more one considers these matters, not in the light of "trick stuff" but as broad concepts of design, the more nearly perfect will be one's "dream ship". In short, barring the quickened motion one must expect in these smaller craft, together with somewhat lessened guest accommodation, one may come close to having the perfect vessel, at least for coastwise cruising.

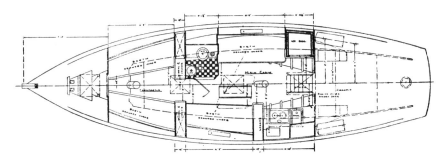

THE CABIN PLAN SHOWS FOREPEAK OF AMPLE SIZE IN WHICH TO STOW MISCELLANEOUS GEAR. THE FORECASTLE IS FITTED WITH TWO FULL SIZE BERTHS, ABAFT WHICH ARE LOCKERS. THE MAIN CABIN IS LARGE AND ARRANGED FOR "LIVABILITY"; GALLEY RANGING IN AN L ACROSS THE AFTER END AS SHOWN. THE TWO BERTHS ARE STAGGERED, THE ONE ON THE PORT HAND BEING FACED BY A DROP LEAF TABLE. TOILET ROOM IS IN THE FORE END OF THE CABIN AND ON THE STARBOARD HAND.

To further the impression of being in a larger vessel, the motion of this particular hull is much dampened in a seaway. This time it is no trick of the eye or fostering of spaciousness, but a characteristic generated from her underbody wherein the center of buoyancy has come forward, somewhat, and thus impedes stamping.

Driven by a sturdy 8 H.P. 2 cylinder 2-cycle Lathrop, relatively heavy for its output, the propeller efficiency at 550 R.P.M.'s gives an actual speed of 5½ knots so that with a fuel capacity of but 28 gallons, the cruising radius is 130 sea miles—enough for any real sailor. Thus the auxiliary weights are kept at a minimum as compared with higher speed reduction-gear installations, and this makes for better sailing which, in turn, calls for less engine use. In passing, I might note that in a flat calm the speed is lowered by half a knot, either from towing the dinghy or allowing the sails to stand.

Of her much disputed rig, at which many have gawked but few

have comprehended, let me say that under its conservative area, quite on the low side when measured in square feet per ton of displacement, or about 70% of the normal spread for her waterline length and relative bulk, she is decidedly smart for a cruising vessel of honest pretensions while there is the added comfort in the ease of handling these small sail units. When sailing alone or "short-handed" with well-meaning but inexperienced duffers who best are battened below in a hard chance, one has not that ever-lurking apprehension of being caught with a main sail to reef or hand. Sail reduction has become a matter of subtraction while she tends herself, close-hauled and a stow or furl that calls for no great haste. Most important, she has that windward ability—weatherliness in its true sense—which is as necessary in a cruising vessel as it is desirable in her racing sister.

She is 33 ft., 4 in. on the waterline, 11 ft., 0 in. in beam, and draws 5 ft., 6 in. Her waterline beam of 10 ft., 2¾ in. belies her apparent chunkiness so that her lines are longish and she has a very easy run. Well salted and ventilated, she was built to last!

In these days, the trend is toward the smaller craft. Go, then, to the designer whose work is to your liking and, for your own well-being afloat, allow him that precious elbow-room so that he may turn out a real "home on the ocean"—however small she may be!

A definition

C. P. Kunhardt

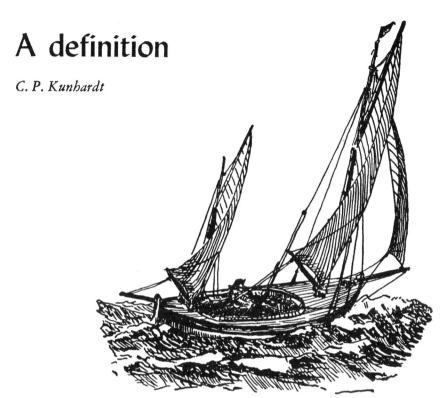

"His ship, his world ~ the rest of
the world, his convenience."

THERE is a peculiar charm in the indefinable feeling of undivided
responsibility to which the single-hand cruiser becomes a willing
slave as he roams over the high seas in his wee barkie, free from
care, far from the harassing annoyances of the world's artificial life, his
own master, in close relations with a boon companion, his ever-ready,
trusty little ship. Though friends be left behind in dusty cities, he finds
a fresh and congenial substitute in the intimate acquaintance of his boat,
for soon he learns to invest his floating home with a personality, caus-
ing the boat's character to appeal to his appreciation as though being
endowed with actual life. He discovers the brave, sturdy qualities his
ship may possess, and approvingly recounts them over and over to himself. He finds she is not perfect, and seeks to correct her weaknesses
and caprices. He handles her tenderly and with care. She becomes the

apple of his eye. There are no "guests" forever asking to be put ashore, wanting to catch an impossible train or boat, nuisances who no sooner board the yacht than their selfish thoughts are concentrated upon the best method of fetching up where they came from. There are no croakers, no nervous lubbers chafing at a few hours' calm, fretting about getting somewhere in the least possible time, as though the yacht were a tiresome prison, and the sea and its ever-changing attractions tasteless for heroes of the barroom, billiard cue, or for dandy knights of the carpet. There are no sideshows under way, no cards down below, no boisterous skylarking under the lee of the mainsail, no store clothes to mar the ideal of amateur life at sea, nothing to interfere with the devotion to the cause and the realization of the dream fancy has perhaps depicted to the longing tar through dreary months of waiting. His ship, his world—the rest of the world, his convenience.

There is no better school for the sailor than the tiny single-hander. Not only does it introduce the amateur to all sorts of work he would escape in larger vessels, and many a practical lesson which might never be learnt but for the demands of cruising alone; but life in these small yachts develops in man or lad an innate love for blue water, a spirit of restless adventure, a longing for "going foreign", which distinguishes the real sailor from the sham article, best described as the "excursionist". The quarters may be cramped, but the necessity of making small room go far affords as an offset great pleasure in seeking by cunning devices and economical planning to circumvent limited space. Serving three meals a day is impossible, but what may be missing in variety, sea air and hard work will make good. Perched upon the weather quarter, peering into the darkness for a landfall after a long day's sail, how grateful then even such commonplace article as a biscuit washed down with a pull at the flask. Not for the finest would one exchange the grateful sensations of such a moment, unknown to any but those who have earned their appetite by serious toil. And then when the mark you have laid your course for all day at last looms through the dark, wet night, and the successful close of your work and care for the day is announced by the racing of the chain through the hawespipe, and the final clink as the turns fall about the bits for a full due—such welcome music from the rattling links sends a thrill of victory to the heart of the weary mariner, to which the trumpeting of a brass band ashore is perfectly insipid. And the cozy feeling of snugness as you find your pet riding quietly under a lee after the rude buffeting of the day, as you push back the slide, light the pretty little cabin lamp below, and start the kettle sizzing for a feast at leisure upon the best your ample, well selected stores afford, topping off with a soothing pipe, all that makes up a combination of bliss unapproached, much less equaled, by anything else ever experienced, in the pursuit of enjoyment.

The mind plans and the body executes. You set yourself a task, and in its accomplishment, above all difficulties, lies your reward. It is play, yet it is work. It is pastime, yet it is a school of instruction. It is theory and practice in the same instant. It is recreation, but also health. It may at times seem like coarse, vulgar work, downright labor, yet its influences are broadening and refining. It may strike the casual ob-

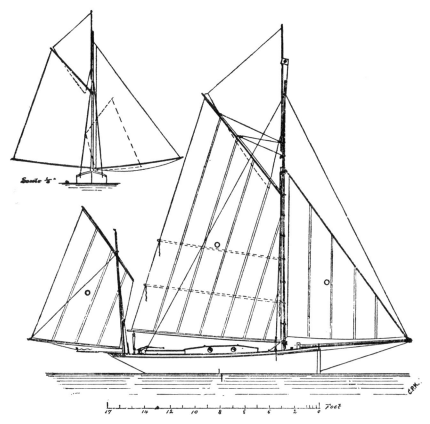

Deuce WAS 17 FT. IN OVER ALL LENGTH; 14 FT. ON THE WATER LINE; 4 FT. 4 IN. IN BREADTH; WITH A DRAFT OF 3 FT. 3 IN.

server as a waste of time. Those who have tried it know better. Even from the sordid standpoint of the money grubber, the time is capital well invested with heavy interest in vigor, boldness, circumspection, and the habit of looking before you leap.

The single-hand cruiser has his annoyances, his disappointments, without doubt, but the endless opportunities for solid, rational enjoyment, study, observation, experiment, and the unlimited range for self-improvement in body and mental capacity, coupled with a dash of romance and the spice of adventure, so far outweigh adverse considerations, that we need not hesitate in counseling the beginner, no matter what his wealth, to start in at the bottom of the ladder, to ship as skipper, crew, and cook aboard the right kind of single-hand yacht, to become a yacht sailor, and more than a mere yacht owner.

In yachts adapted to a special purpose certain predominating considerations govern the design, and to them all others must be considered subordinate. In judging of a design or in fixing upon a selection, these chief objectives must be kept in view. In the plans of *Deuce,* certain peculiarities were aimed at in connection with the general requirements expected of all varieties of boats. The single-hand yacht is to be in main a floating home. She is to be a small edition in most respects of a large yacht, so that the same sort of sport and concomitant benefits may be enjoyed, though on a smaller scale and at a tithe of the expense. Such boats must be cheap; small, in fact as small as it is possible to make them answer the intended purpose. They must be safe, absolutely so, not only probably so. They must be under easy control, possess permanent accommodations, be firm to face bad weather, and as able as their limited size permits. In these aesthetic days they must be handsome and smart looking, too, with a finish attractive to the eye.

The size is regulated to a great extent, perhaps altogether, by the tape-line dimensions of the proposed occupant and the mark at which he brings down the scales—for a heavy weight a large boat, for a light weight a smaller one; but in each individual case the smallest suitable to the person. The underlying idea with the lonely voyager is to get the most out of the least boat. It is always possible that he may be able to sail a much larger yacht; but that is just what he does not want, for that means more expense to start with—more for keep, more work, and more draft, to say nothing of the ever-present insidious temptation "to take a friend along". Now, nothing can be more heretical and schis-

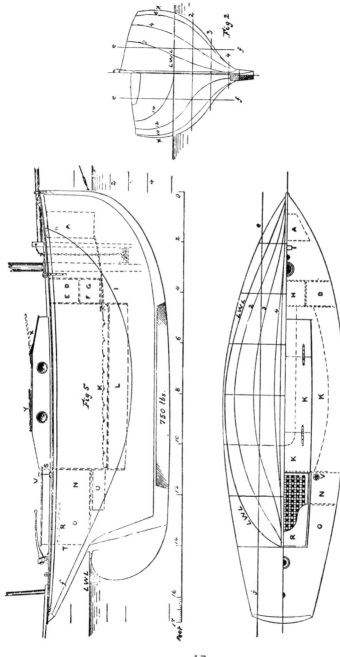

DRAWINGS OF THE LINES WITH THE BODY PLAN, DECK AND CABIN ARRANGEMENT OF THE SINGLE-HANDER *Deuce.* BERTH FOR ONE IS SHOWN ON THE PORT HAND WITH A HINGED TABLE OPPOSITE. THE GALLEY IS TUCKED UNDER THE FORWARD DECK.

matic to the true orthodox and respectable faith of the single-hander than the division of the pleasures of his cruise with some barbarian of another school, not in full sympathy and a devout follower of the same creed. The greatest independence, the gratification of self, and accountability to no one, constitute the main attractions of a cruise all alone. To divide with an intruder is to become a passenger and a slave to the inclinations of others—afflictions impregnated with bitter gall if, in addition, the "friend" chews up your smooth, white decks with hobnail boots, innocently shipped for the occasion, spills grease about the boat, litters up the cockpit, and rams the yawl's head against your beauty's glistening side till she has the appearance of suffering from small-pox, keeping your teeth on edge in expectation of the next piece of savagery to which the boat is to become a victim.

When the single-hander wants a friend and companion, the only satisfactory method is to take him along in a boat of his own, and thus obtain gregarious conviviality in squadron, not in one confined cabin. Moreover, he has a right to expect as much, for if the friend be really a lover of yachting and not an "excursionist" imbued with a passing impulse, the bane of true yachtsmen, the friend can so easily acquire his own little boat, that it is nothing less than imposing upon good nature to break in upon the singlehander's charmed circle where only berthing for one has been contemplated. At all events this is the interpretation the devotees of sailing alone puts upon the sport as he follows it. For all that no one, not even the most inveterate admirer of small boat sailing, will deny the pleasures of cruising in larger craft with company aboard, but they say men differ in their tastes, and yachtsmen are human. Give unto Caesar what is Caesar's, and give to the single-hander his solitary seclusion aboard his own ship, or he is not quite happy. His boat must be for him and he for his boat. Nothing less than that will do. Those unwilling to subscribe to his doctrine have no business building a single-hander, but should go in for tonnage enough to lug along Tom, Dick and Harry, and build of cast iron to meet the inroads from a promiscuous horde, with hob nails, store clothes, fastidious appetites and particular trains to catch. Perhaps sailing alone is a little selfish, but that makes it all the more enticing this side of the millennium.

Written in 1887 by the late Mr. C. P. Kunhardt
and reprinted from SMALL YACHTS by the kind permission of
the proprietors, FIELD & STREAM.

Tabloid cruising cutter

Designed by Allan Clarkson

THE design, shown on these pages was left with us a good many years ago by Mr. Allan Clarkson, of Exeter, N. H. The little cruiser was for his own enjoyment—drawn on his own time—and to his own particular requirements. There were no "monkeys, devils or hyenas," to quote Mr. L. Francis Herreshoff, who could stick their "oars" into his work.

While, to our knowledge, the boat has never been built she does incorporate many attractive features. There is one thing we are not sure of. It is apparent the designer was in doubt whether or not he would like a cutter or a sloop. The sail plan shows a cutter rig while his lines and arrangement show mast stepping for a sloop. Never-the-less the resulting design is most pleasing to the eye.

The sailplan is simple and straightforward. There are no unnecessary struts, spreaders or shrouds. A single shroud each side, with a single headstay and jibstay will provide sufficient stiffness to the spar, a system of rigging that has stood the test of time. The shrouds lead far enough aft to make runners or a permanent backstay unnecessary. while the boom may not pay out quite as far as it might, in running before the wind, the advantages of eliminating the runners or permanent backstay more than compensate for that fault.

The sails are divided into proportionate areas. With a double reef in the main and the staysail standing good balance will be maintained. A reaching jib is shown which may prove advantageous at times. The mainsail has an area of 175 sq. ft. and the staysail has an area of 58 sq. ft. making a total of 233 sq. ft. in the two working sails. And additional 57 sq. ft. in the jib brings up the total sail area to 290 sq. ft. This is ample sail area for a boat of this kind.

The deck arrangement of the 20 foot tabloid cruising cutter has been given careful consideration in the matter of praticability. With the exception of the access hatch and the bowsprit the foredeck is clear and excellent space is shown for the stowage of the anchor and other ground tackle. The mast, in being stepped through the raised deck, and

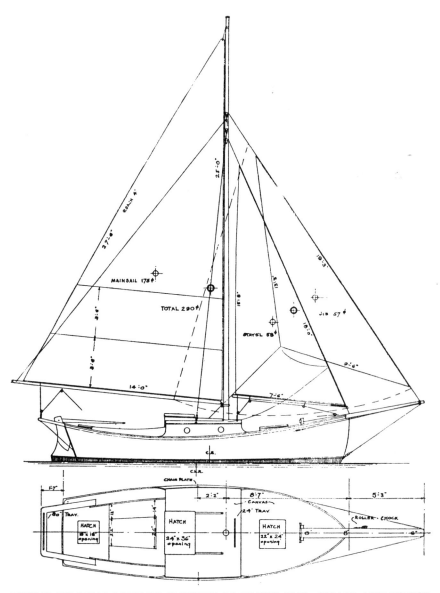

THIS IS AN IDEAL SORT OF CRUISING BOAT FOR ONE. SMALL AND SIMPLE THEREFORE A MINIMUM OF CARE IS REQUIRED IN KEEPING HER SHIP-SHAPE. HER SAILPLAN AND DECK ARRANGEMENT HAVE BEEN GIVEN CAREFUL CONSIDERATION IN ACHIEVING ATTRACTIVENESS AND PRAC-TICABILITY.

20

staysail traveler, located as shown, eliminate many lines and blocks
m the forward deck. In rough weather one can go forward through
cabin, thereby not running any risk of falling overboard while
ssing the raised deck. The latter is a dangerous arrangement on a
ll boat and one that should be carefully considered before it is in-
porated in the design. In connection with this it may be interesting
note that while low bulwarks may not give sure protection they do
e an apparent feeling of security and do provide safe footing each
e of a trunk cabin boat. As an extra precaution rail stanchions may
installed on either raised deck or trunk cabin boats.

A short bridgedeck furnishes the necessary arrangement for a wa-
ight, self bailing cockpit, and gives strength to the hull. And the
mings, extending from the raised deck, give one a feeling of securi-
nd of being "in" the boat rather than "on" it. Cockpit seats, either
e of the boat, are 14 in. wide at the forward end and 12 in. wide at
stern. These seats are set lower than the main deck and are flush
h the bridgedeck, which is also several inches below the main deck.
s arrangement also lowers people in the cockpit. The hatch on the
r deck gives access to the lazarette.

The results of the time spent on the drawing of the lines is appar-
because they are well thought out The principal dimensions of the
t are as follows: 20 ft. 0 in. overall, 18 ft 4½ in. on the waterline,
. 6 in. breadth and a draft of 4 ft. 0 in. The body plan is exceptional-
interesting and graceful; the sections show ample breadth at W. L. 4
viding plenty of width for the cabin floor without unduly increasing
displacement. The waterlines are well balanced and should produce
deal little cruising boat. Her full deck line has the advantages of
viding additional space on deck and also forms a slight flare on her
ides forward: this will tend to keep her decks dry while the sheer-
is particularly "cocky" and pleasing.

Construction indicated is moderately heavy. The keel will be made
ellow pine 8 in. by 12 in. It will be shaped as shown, the forward
being tapered to fair into the 4 in. stem, and the after end to fair
vith the stern post and deadwood. The iron keel weighs 2,100 lbs.
will be bolted to the keel with six galvanized iron bolts ⅞ in. in
The forward and after bolts will be on the center line; the other
staggered 2 in. either side the center line.

The frames will be made of white oak, steam bent 1¼ in. by 1½
nd set on 9 in. centers. First class boat building practice calls for

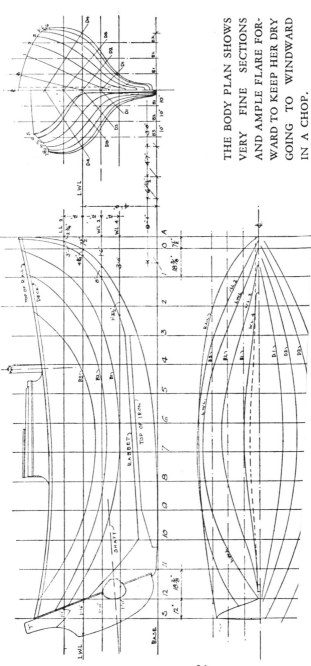

THE BODY PLAN SHOWS VERY FINE SECTIONS AND AMPLE FLARE FORWARD TO KEEP HER DRY GOING TO WINDWARD IN A CHOP.

21

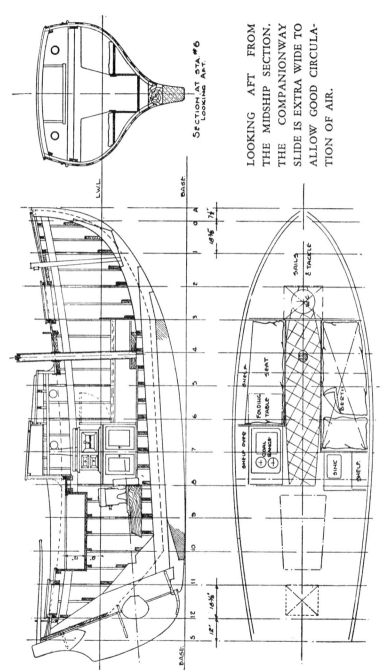

SECTION AT STA. #6
LOOKING AFT.

LOOKING AFT FROM THE MIDSHIP SECTION. THE COMPANIONWAY SLIDE IS EXTRA WIDE TO ALLOW GOOD CIRCULATION OF AIR.

THE ARRANGEMENT PLAN AGAIN SHOWS SIMPLICITY. A SINGLE BERTH TO STARBOARD WILL CAUSE YOU TO THINK TWICE BEFORE INVITING SOME "KNIGHT OF THE BAR ROOM" OR "NERVOUS LUBBER CHAFING AT A FEW HOURS' CALM" TO COME ABOARD.

23

these to be mortised into the sides of the keel, deadwood and stem. The floor timbers will be made of 1¼ in. thick white oak; one set on each frame, as indicated. The shelf will be sawn from ⅞ in. by 4 in. fir tapered slightly at the ends. Planking will be ⅞ in. white cedar laid with at least 17 strakes each side of the keel. The deck beams will be made of ⅞ in. by 2 in. white oak set on the same centers as the frames. The raised deck beams may be of lesser dimensions. Both main and raised deck will be made of ⅞ in. by 3 in. tongue and groove white pine and covered with canvas.

The cabin is laid out very simply. A watercloset may be installed forward, under the access hatch; the former is a piece of useful or useless equipment; which is again a matter of personal opinion. As Mr. Hanks has said, "different ships, different long splices;" so there you have it; you be the judge. A full length berth to starboard provides comfortable accommodations for one to sleep. Possibly Mr. Clarkson has also read Mr. Kunhardt and reached the conclusion that "one is enough." It may be that solitude may be a burden to some and quite agreeable to others.

The designer shows a seat, opposite the single berth, which is fitted with a small hinged table at the after end. Evidently he is a man looking for solid comfort when living on a small boat. A model 1011 Shipmate range will be installed in the galley. This little range is the smallest made and is 21¾ in. long by 15 in. deep and 16 in. high. It weighs only 103 lbs. Opposite the range there is a small sink, shelf and cupboard.

In his design Mr. Clarkson has managed to obtain full headroom, under the raised deck, and yet maintain pleasing appearance. The companionway slide is extra wide to allow circulation of air over the galley and it also opens up the after end of the cabin.

Powered with a Universal Fisherman engine, having 67 cu. in. cylinder displacement, the little cutter should slide along at a good 7 miles an hour.

Mr. Garboard.

Cruise in the rain

John J. Pflieger

I HAVE just come back from a two-day sail, and feel as if I had been away for a month, which proves that although I didn't have much sleep or rest, it is just the change I required from the office routine. I decided to play "hooky" from the office for half a day on Saturday; so, at 8 P.M. on Friday night, I was off to the boatyard with my bundles on my back and yachting cap at a jaunty angle.

After getting all my stuff on board, including sleeping bag and hammock; bailing the boat out; rigging her and checking everything up —it was 10 P.M. when I set sail, against the tide of course, and with only a moderate breeze, a light Southwester. What prompted my leaving, rather than spend the night at the mooring to get an early start the next day, was that the gnats near shore were making things rather uncomfortable for me, what with my bare knees and shorts. They are really worse than mosquitoes; they raised big welts on my legs, arms and neck, and would even play hide and seek in the hair sticking out of my ears.

Getting out of the harbor was not easier than usual, with the back-wind from the big trees, the contrary tide, and of course the usual ferry in my way, just when about to tack. The result was that, notwithstanding the vigorous use of paddles, I found myself stuck hard on a rock, near the Glen Island Casino, with the crooner putting in a mocking note from his saxophone (a kind of Bronx cheer, which certainly must have been meant for me). As it was quite dark, with only a sliver of a moon out, it was not till 11 P.M. that I was safely out, past Beckwith Beach, listening to Taps coming from Fort Slocum—time for all good soldiers to go to bed, but for all brave sailors to venture out.

Instead of sailing S.W. towards the shelter of City Island, where I would have been nearer Port Washington, my ultimate goal, I had to go the other way with the help of the tide. By midnight, I was anchored near Huckleberry Island, ready to go to sleep. However, fate decided otherwise. A strong N.N.E. wind began to blow, and as I was too near shore for safety in case my anchor started to drag, I decided to head for Execution Rock and the general direction of Port Washington.

The stars soon began to disappear, the sky taking a beautiful hue, like that of a black pearl, which soon changed into the color of pea soup; and a light drizzle came down. So I added to my shorts, long trousers and a T-shirt, another sweater and a raincoat. Then fortified myself with a cup of coffee and the cheese and crackers I had rescued from a cocktail party at home. The sailing seemed slow, as I probably still had the tide against me. I had passed the Execution Rock Lighthouse and was in the main channel with large cargo boats going by. They probably could not see my little oil lamp fluttering at the top of my jib, so that I tried to lash my electric lamp on the mainsail, giving it a ghostlike appearance in the mist.

Drifting from red-flashing to fixed green light buoys and vice-versa, I finally turned around Sands Point on Long Island, dropping the anchor near a beach, well in the lee and protected from the N.E. It was 4 A.M. when I went to sleep, and a faint glow was already appearing in the East.

At 6:30 A.M. I was awakened, much to my disgust, by faint putt! putts!, becoming ever louder. The usual early fishermen pleasure-bent! They must have been a mile off, but I could hear their arguments as plainly as if they had been with me under the canvas of the boom. After that, I only dozed off, and finally got up at 7:30 A.M., when fruit, eggs sunnyside-up, crackers and cheese, toast and marmalade, coffee and a cigarette set me in good humor for the rest of the day. Then I hoisted sail again, passing close to the cabanas and the white sand beach of Sands Point Casino.

The day was bright, the sun up, and a light N.N.E. was blowing still, enabling me to sail on a broad reach, amongst the 50 and 60-footers, which seemed ready to go out on a race, as a committee boat was on hand. I knew that Don was having a vacation, and I hoped to find his beach club from a vague description he gave me at lunch some four or five weeks before. So I tied up to a long dock, where a six-year old boy eyed me approvingly, who later took complete possession of my boat. I managed to call up Don's wife from the Port Washington Yacht Club next door: "No, they didn't belong to the club I had tied up to. No, they could not go sailing with me Sunday, because they were going to Jones Beach." Well, I gave them a rain check. They would have needed it anyway, as it poured buckets all day, despite the Weather Bureau prediction: "Strong South wind of about 35 miles intensity and scattered showers."

The strong Southerly came while I was eating lunch at anchor, not far from the beach club, in a setting of small boats—one at least of my class, a Winabout.

SO I TIED UP TO A LONG DOCK, WHERE A SIX YEAR OLD BOY EYED ME AP-
PROVINGLY, WHO LATER TOOK COMPLETE POSSESSION OF MY BOAT.

I lifted the hook in the early afternoon, making sail for what I found out was Louie's Restaurant, "Sea Food Specialty." From there I 'phoned George, who "would be pleased to come for a sail with his wife"—after I gave him a thumbnail description of what to wear. The Southern breeze was strong and it was cloudy; but good sailing weather, especially in the Bay. We looked for *Vabel III*, a friend's yacht; but it didn't appear to be moored where it had been last season, and I could not remember whether it was a sloop or a yawl. Sunday evening the next day, I almost bumped into it: it was a sloop. The yawl, I then recalled, was a boat he'd had in Belgium, of which he had showed me photographs. We sailed on with just our main, the jib down, blowing into the water until rolled up and properly secured. We were on the King's Point side of the bay, opposite the spot where I had spent the night before. My crew insisted on rounding the point to look at one of their friends' estate, which was always the "one after this one." The water in this unprotected part was quite rough, especially as I did not want to sail too close to shore without looking at my charts.

Kings Point is where I broke my rudder track the season before in a similar breeze and strong tide which beached me before I could drop my anchor. So I consider the Point as a hoodoo, and sure enough my track broke again, and the bottom of my rudder was entirely loose. I must have damaged it on the rocks the night before, loosening the screws, and the strong blow finished the job. We sailed the boat as best we could without pushing her too hard, with George managing the mainsail in an understanding manner for a landlubber, and I holding the rudder with one hand, and the tiller with the other.

We made the dock with a bang, which was unavoidable as I couldn't point the *Tomojac* well with the loose rudder, and before I could get up forward or let the sail down (having to jump over several pairs of legs) we had backed away. The main, which came down, was wrapped around the tiller, and in my hurry to prevent a tear, I unloosed the tiller pin and saw my rudder disappear in the murky mud. I tried to mark the spot with a cross-bearing with my left arm, and grab some rowboat or some mooring with my right hand. We soon found out it was useless to try to row against the wind, and the Lord only knows how the string of Louie's rowboats were all tied to one another but could not get us back to shore. I was afraid to untie one as there were no floats on the lines, and I feared to lose his mooring. Finally, we hailed one of those nondescript powerboats, aptly called a one-lunger, I believe. He gave us a tow for those few yards, having quite a time as his engine went dead twice, coughing like an asthmatic old woman.

George seemed rather displeased that I didn't accept his dinner invitation; but I wanted to watch the tide and try to recuperate my lost rudder at low tide. So I tidied the boat up, put the high boomcrotch up which Jack made me at school, allowing the use of a high canvas for an easy night on board. At 7 P.M. Louie's dining room was already crowded, and although I found a table, I could not get waited on—with the usual war shortage of help—till 9 o'clock! By that time I was asleep, sitting erect at the table, dead from only three hours sleep the night before. But after dinner I felt better, and had the joy, when I walked out on the strongly-lit boardwalk, to find my rudder sticking out of the water like a diminutive dinosaur. I hit the hammock peacefully, and slept like a log, only half-conscious of occasional banging of rowboats against my hull, notwithstanding my fenders, and of a steady rain, which seemed after a while to trickle on the port side and find its way into the lowest part of my hammock where the heaviest part of my anatomy rested.

It was Sunday morning. I woke up out of habit at 7 A.M., well rested. The rain had subsided, but the sky looked threatening and a strong S.W. breeze was still blowing. I fixed breakfast. Couldn't have peaches and cream—or rather milk—because my thermos bottle poured forth buttermilk, due to the storm and constant rolling of the boat. So I compromised on plums, fried fillet of soles with lemon, crackers and marmalade, coffee and my usual cigarette.

As I had found out the afternoon before, (when I purchased a new jute jib sheet and a new mop) that the marine store had little fittings left and no spare bronze tracks, I knew that I had to rely on a rope to hold my rudder up. And I didn't feel that I should venture out in that blow to cross over to New Rochelle. So I sat on the dock, facing some boatyard, and began a watercolor; it was still unfinished, when I went on board the *Tomojac* to avoid the rain. I had a drink, lunch, coffee, a cigar, took a nap, read TIME, and started another watercolor painting. This was facing the Port Washington Public Docks, with the W.E.A.F. radio pylons in the distance, all done during a steady and unending downpour. Only occasionally did it drizzle; it came down mostly in buckets. Once in a while a sailboat would pass my stern before making the dock; the crews were soaked through and through. A small sailboat pulled alongside; two captains, U.S.A., and a Lieutenant Commander, with a civilian skipper, probably the owner. They had crossed over from New Rochelle, and all looked like water rats. Waiting until

WE HAILED A NONDESCRIPT POWER BOAT; IT GAVE US A TOW FOR THOSE
FEW YARDS, HAVING QUITE A TIME AS ITS ENGINE WENT DEAD, COUGH-
ING LIKE AN ASTHMATIC OLD WOMAN.

the rain moderated somewhat, I put on a sou'wester and walked over
to Louie's bar to have a drink like the others.

There I killed the time sketching some people. Most looked like
yachtsmen, all had been wet. One man came in whom I knew from
downtown New York; he was not sailing, just lived nearby, and was
dressed in shorts, a custom probably acquired in India, where he had
spent some years. After an early supper I found that it had finally
stopped raining.

I hoisted my reefed mainsail; my rudder was supported by a thin
cotton rope, and I left Port Washington at 8 P.M. A Southwest wind
was still blowing, but not too strong (possibly a 5 Beaufort, a fresh
breeze). While I was watching my rudder, the *Tomojac* pointed into
the wind, and I just missed a boat, the *Vabel III*. Later, my rudder
had slipped, and I made for a large schooner with a dinghy on a painter,
and tied up to it. But before I could finish, the owner was on deck. He
was understanding, like the average boat fraternity member. Only a
few words: "I am in trouble!" I threw him a line and he tied me up;

30

tightening the rope around the rudder I inserted my foghorn underneath it so as to be able to adjust the tension should it slacken; that did the trick, and carried me to my mooring.

Another big yacht under power, hailed, gave me the tide, as I did not want to lose time and needed to allow for drifting. Sailing on a broad reach all the way home, I only changed sides once in a while; but sitting mostly on the lee side under my boom to starboard. By 10:30 P.M. I had moored the boat, but found it took me another hour to straighten out things in the dark, and pump my rowboat out; another half-hour or so to find room to tie my rowboat to the dock, as it is so crowded that one's own space at the end of a week-end is invariably taken, and one has to untie and displace half a dozen dinghies before finding a place to squeeze in. That is just one aggravation to a week-end cruise, which gives one a bad taste, but for which I have been unable to find a solution. Just one of those things to make people at home wonder if you drowned, and make them call up the Coast Guard to hunt you up. I understand that this is quite frequently being done since night-sailing has been resumed, only to find the corpse playing poker in some cozy nook with the boys, while his wife is having all kinds of fits at home. It probably serves her right! She should go along and sail too!

EMETT

"Just like them to go and spoil the amenities with a block of flats."

Reproduced from PUNCH
by kind permission of
the proprietors.

A Seabright skiff
goes inland

THE original Seabright skiff is a round bilge open boat and has been used for many years by the fishermen living along the New Jersey coast line. And because these boats have a very good reputation for ability to work in rough water tending pound nets and hand-lining they, naturally, have been found useful in places far away from the exposed beaches where they were first built and used, and for other uses than fishing.

The plans of the little open boat illustrating these notes is a Seabright skiff; this one, however, is of V-bottom model, but otherwise has all the characteristics of the originals of the Jersey shore-line. It was designed by Atkin & Co., Darien, Conn., for Mr. James S. Maze of Peru, Illinois and when built will be used at his summer home on one of the large Wisconsin lakes.

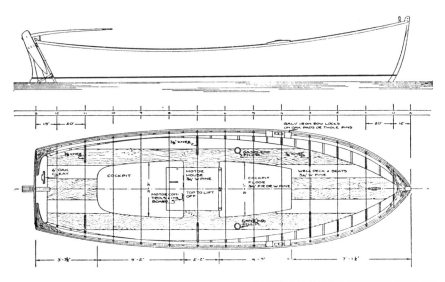

THE DECK ARRANGEMENT SHOWS TWO COCKPITS WITH ENGINE HOUSE BETWEEN. THE SEATS ARE CONTINUOUS AND ARE SET WELL DOWN IN THE HULL.

The boat has an overall length of 22 ft. 3 in.; a water line length of 20 ft.; a breadth of 6 ft. 10 in.; and a draft of 1 ft. 5½ in. The freeboard at the bow is, 3 ft. 7 in. and at the stern, 2 ft. 5 in., so one can see she is, for her length, a very big boat.

The plan view shows a unique arrangement. There is no deck; simply open gunwales with proper breast hook forward and well formed quarter knees aft. The seats are continuous from bow to stern and are set well below the line of the sheer. Leg room is provided by the two cockpits as shown. With such an arrangement one may stretch out in comfort or sit with back against the gunwale and find comfort. The engine will be installed under a house a little abaft amidships, and by the way, will not be the two cylinder unit shown in the plans; but a

THE SECTIONS OF THIS PARTICU-
LAR SEABRIGHT SKIFF ARE OF V
BOTTOM FORM; THIS BEING AN
ATKINIZED DEVELOPMENT OF
THESE EXCELLENT SEA-GOING
BOATS.

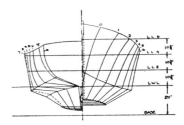

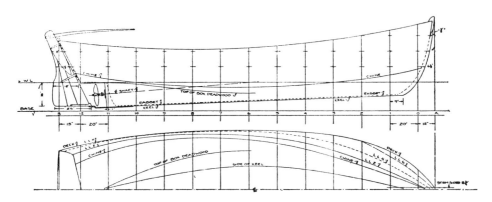

THE LINES SHOW THE TYPICAL BOX DEADWOOD OF THE FAMOUS SEA-BRIGHT SKIFF; THE LONG FLAT STRAIGHT KEEL, THE PERFECTLY PRO-TECTED RUDDER AND PROPELLER, AND THE VERY SMALL ANGULARITY OF THE SHAFT.

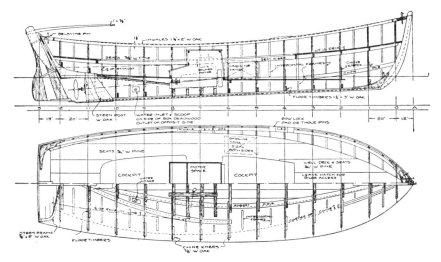

THE CONSTRUCTION PLAN OF THE V BOTTOM BOAT SHOWS THE CORRECT
WAY IN WHICH TO BUILD A BOAT; NO PLYWOODS, PLASTICS, ROT-PROOF-
ING, OR OTHER DOUBTFUL MATERIALS BEING SPECIFIED. WHAT CAN BE
BETTER FOR BOAT BUILDING THAN THE HONEST AND PROVEN MATERI-
ALS USED IN THE PAST?

Graymarine Sea Scout. The expected speed is eight miles an hour.
Rather than a steering wheel, which has no place on this kind of ship,
a handy long tiller will be used; a simple, very practical and positive
method of steering any kind of small boat.

The construction of the 22 footer is after the manner of the sturdy
little boats that were built over thirty years ago. All the proper parts
are included and these in the places they must be if the boat as a whole
is to give long and satisfactory service. Like the designers of Mr. Maze's
boat, your writer does not believe there are any modern short cuts in
boatbuilding that compare in any manner with the meticulous workmanship of workmen who, beginning in their early teens, learned the
trade by working long hours under the guidance of masters of the
craft. It just may be that workmen today do not work long enough
hours to learn the trades they profess to know; at any rate there are all
too few skilled workmen today.

Mr. Ratline

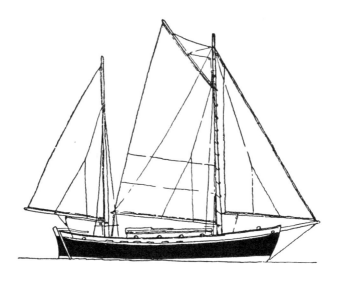

Carcassonne
John G. Hanna

Efficiency versus adequacy

John G. Hanna

MOST boating books and magazines of today are at least 51 per cent bunk. And the most buncombilious bunk of all they contain is this w.k. "efficiency" bleat. Now efficiency is a good thing in its place, and that place is anything having to do with the getting of money. The most efficient factory is the one which produces bologna sausage, or washing machines, or near-silk sox, or what have you, at least cost. The most efficient machine is the one that turns out the most thousand of boxes of matches, or bottles of coke, per hour, with least operative expense. And the most efficient boat is the one that produces the greatest amount of gold and silver cups and cash prizes per season.

36

You simply can't analyze this efficiency talk in any guise you ever find it without sooner or later running up against the almighty dollar.

Now far be it from me to decry the dollar. I am a dollar chaser myself, to the best of my limited ability, and it is a source of profound grief to me that the darned things seem always able to keep about two jumps ahead of me in spite of my most desperate efforts. The only people who ever speak slightingly of dollar chasers are the pound, mark, franc and lira chasers, grabbers, squeezers and holders. And even these people stop knocking and save their breath for a desperate dive after dollars whenever any such coins appear in their vicinity. In fact, with the immense tide of American travel now flowing to Europe, dollar chasing promises to displace political intrigue and general belliaking as the favorte sport of our European cousins.

If a man becomes such a slave to dollar chasing that he cannot possibly think or enjoy life in any other terms, of course he must buy only the most "efficient" obtainable boat, to be happy. But there are many who can and do leave every commercial idea at the office and take up some hobby for pleasure, and pleasure alone. If that hobby is boating, the pleasure comes in being afloat, away from the land and its harassing problems, free from all worry and care, and above all, free from the ceaseless compulsion to get somewhere on schedule time, which is the worst characteristic of American life. A good boat for such a man must be fully adequate for such use, and if it is not, it is a failure, no matter if it is the most "efficient" craft ever designed.

A famous passage in a forgotten book tells about a stupid young man who was knocked down by a big dog belonging to a young girl both beautiful and wise (never mind, any combination can be found in books). "What kind of dog is that? Of what use is he?" peevishly demanded the s.y.m. "Why, he isn't a *use* dog. He's just a *pleasure* dog," retorted the b.y.g. Now what this country needs is more just pleasure boats. If it takes a 150-pound St. Bernard dog to please a young lady, she should have it, and if it takes a heavy-hulled ketch to please a certain man, he should buy that boat, for no other will ever satisfy him.

Speed is certainly no detriment, in itself. Other things being equal, the faster boat is preferable. The hell of it is, other things are *never* equal. Once a man begins to sacrifice this and that for speed, there is no stopping him until he has sold his very soul to the devil for the last possible 1/64th of a mile per hour, and instead of a boat, he has a work-house and a worry-farm.

The best boat, as I see it, is the one most fully adequate to all that comes up day by day when one sets out to seek relaxation and pleasure afloat. She should be strong and tight above all things, and heavily timbered, because there is no peace in a light, corky hull forever tossing about. She should be buoyant and dry, for wet crews make for illness and ill temper. She should have a great ability to mind her business and take care of herself, for it wears a man down to have to con and coax a boat every minute and pull her out of tight corners by main strength and sweat. It doesn't matter a particle whether she has an "efficient" sail plan. Any rig her owner likes to work with is the best rig. Nor is the last yelp in super-powerful gasoline burners at all essential. Any old engine her owner understands and gets faithful service from is the correct power plant. And the only interior detail that really matters is a full man's sized, actual, practicable working model of a galley, for indigestion has wrecked more cruises than rocks and hurricanes.

That's the kind of boat I like to read about, and it is the kind which this series of books, as I understand it, is designed to encourage.

Boats that are highly efficient machines and highly productive mug-hunters are doubtless all right in their way and their place—so are fleas. We can safely leave it to some of our efficient and ebullient contemporaries to boost that kind of boat. I hope this will be simply the book of *adequate* boats—boats that are adequate to all the moods and occasions of the sea, and all the needs of men afloat; anti-fret, fuss, sweat and worry boats; purely pleasure boats; boats that are all boat and all there; boats beautiful with the simple harmony of line and proportion that even the most heavy and rugged can have; and "efficiency" be damned!

This delightful essay was written and published a quarter
century ago; and the idea it heralds is as true
today as it was when dear old J. G. H. of
HEAVING THE LEAD fame
wrote it in 1926.

Three studies in profile and arrangement

John Atkin

THE outboard profiles and arrangements of the 37 ft., 0 in. by 36 ft., 0 in. by 10 ft., 10 in. by 2 ft., 9½ in. power boat shown on these pages are to illustrate three ways of going about securing a suitable arrangement for a client's particular needs or requirements.

I have drawn the finished lines of an Atkinized hull and then, with careful calculations, gone about the task of producing a boat which would satisfy her prospective owner.

The question of where and what a boat is to be used for is, quite naturally, an essential one. A shallow draft boat for use on the Great South Bay of Long Island would not be practical to use down East. Nor would a Jersey sea skiff be suitable for, perhaps, Pudget Sound. For the particular make of land, shoals, bays, etc. determines the type of boat best suited for that vicinity. It is for that reason various boats are developed all over the world; the dhow, the Norwegian double-enders, the sampans, the Jersey sea skiffs, the Chesapeake Bay bugeyes, the New Haven sharpies, the Friendship sloops and a list veritably a mile in length.

This particular hull was designed for a cruising man at Schenectady, N. Y. and is to be used around the lock, canal and lake country of upper New York State. Albany will possibly be her home port. Cruises down the Hudson, to Lake Champlain, up to the Great Lakes, etc., necessitate a wholesome boat that will safely carry her crew through all weather conditions and still be of reasonable draft.

These three studies, Nos. 1, 2 and 3, adaptable to the same hull, all have their own particular advantages and disadvantages. These factors I will take up one by one and compare each to illustrate just what to look for when you go about having a boat designed or when buying a stock hull.

At this point possibly the question of changes arises; of altering weights; materials, etc. My father has, for these past many years, again and again told his Shipmates, "not to change the beam, the draft, the height of the cockpit floor, the main cabin floor, the specified type of engine or the weights, etc." His advice is very sound. The slightest alteration, which in itself seems non-essential, will later bring about a series of problems which will be difficult to solve.

In actuality these are three entirely different boats, studies Nos. 1, 2 and 3. The hull alone is similar. Basic calculations have been made to determine the position of the primary weights, including trimming ballast. Location of the engine, the tanks, the stove, the batteries, etc. was taken into consideration when the layout was prepared.

Upon close study and a good deal of thought, talks with the owner's wife, varied experts, and his own opinion, the owner returned the three sketches. In all probability features of each design appealed to the owner. When these features are all thrashed out a design will be prepared which will exactly suit his requirements.

Without the services of industrial streamliners of ice boxes, radios, fountain pens, door knobs, typewriters or electric fans (God bless their streamlined souls) we have produced, I believe, three designs which are not ugly and which combine the utmost in practicability, ship-shape-ness with a great deal of grace and beauty.

Having tremendous esteem for such fine experienced naval architects as L. Francis Herreshoff, Albert W. Crouch, John Hacker, Milo Bailey and the late William H. Hand, Jr., Charles D. Mower, W. P. Stephens and W. H. Patterson and with them in mind I prepared these designs.

There is no bath-tub stern, nor raking stern inviting water to come aboard when going astern or running in a following sea, nor plastic planks, nor rounded dangerous deck edges, nor plywood, nor wet convex sections forward, nor rounded stem, nor plastic windshields nor any other features borrowed from the "post-war cruiser."

In this boat we have a fine deck, 22 inches in width around the deck houses, with a high bulwark rail to prevent small and large members of the crew from tumbling overboard. The deck houses are strong and fitted with practical crown and sides. The hull will behave herself in rough weather and will slide through the water at a real 13 miles an hour with a medium duty Red Wing "Arrow Super Six" of 404 cu. in. cylinder displacement at 1600 R.P.M., or a Kermath "Seacaptain" six with 495 cu. in. displacement, at 1600 R.P.M. Neither of these installations will be equipped with reduction gears.

In these three designs I feel we are a little ahead of the times. There is gracefulness and beauty in each. If the double cabin model

No. 3, doesn't give the appearance of speed you can be assured that her lack of "streamlining" will not prevent her from moving through the water at a speed equal to the other two.

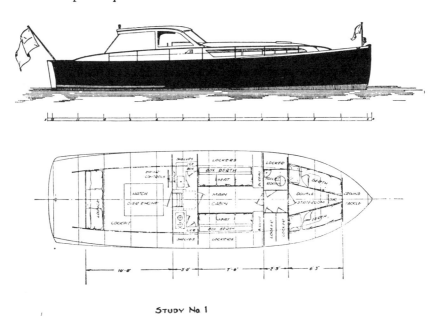

STUDY No. 1

THE PROFILE OF STUDY NO. 1 SHOWS A MODERN TREATMENT OF THE ATKIN DESIGNED 36 FT. CRUISER. WITH SIDE DECKS OF GENEROUS WIDTH AND STANCHION RAILINGS, THE MATTER OF GOING FORWARD IS MADE SAFE.

The trunk cabin model, No. 1, is the most practical in regard to using the widest part of the hull for accommodations. She is unusually low and trim looking. Her engine controls and steering wheel are fairly far aft which is a common position for handling such a boat and is a popular steering position.

Forward there is space for lines and other ground tackle. Her deck here is spacious enough to take care of two light anchors and there is room to handle these comfortably and therefore picking up a mooring from her full deck will not be difficult.

Abaft the ground tackle compartment are two single berths. Each of these is 6 ft. 3 in. long and 2 ft. 6 in. wide. Forward, between them,

41

is a bureau in which to stow clothes and miscellaneous dunnage. Under each berth are large lockers.

The toilet room, situated as it is, provides easy access from either stateroom. There will not be any need to pass through cabins to reach it. A large locker on the starboard hand is divided into two, one for each stateroom.

The hatch in the trunk cabin top will allow access to the forward deck and it is placed directly over the passageway amidship.

The main cabin is provided with two full length seats. Pullman-type box berths are outboard of these. This arrangement has a great advantage. The seats are strictly for sitting on. The berths to sleep in. A couch or lounge, when constantly sat on, is sure to become lumpy and out of shape which causes uncomfortable resting. By using box berths this condition is avoided. The berths can be made up all the time with two or three wide canvas straps across the bed clothes to prevent their becoming crumpled and will allow them always to be ready for sleeping. Stowage space for blankets, sheets, etc., is taken care of in the berth. No need to unfold steering seats, luncheonettes, chart tables, etc. Just two plain, sensible berths which are comfortable and convenient.

The main cabin is fitted with bureaus to port and starboard with lockers outboard of the box berths. These lockers will be high enough to hang suits and coats.

The galley is well situated for a good many reasons. Coming in out of wet weather it provides a good place to remove rain gear. It is naturally well ventilated by the wide companion way. The full beam of the boat is used and more room is available athwartship which consequently reduces the fore and aft dimension. It is placed so as to allow food to be passed to the cockpit where many meals are eaten.

There is 6 ft. 3 in. headroom throughout the cabins of each of these studies. More could be gained by higher deck houses or lowering the floor without destroying their appearances. Few people, however, have to do any ducking with such headroom.

The standing top covers two thirds of the cockpit, which allows sunshine to enter and lends better proportion to the boats appearance. If desired, revolving fishing chairs may be installed. The lounge being so far aft has one particular disadvantage. Fumes from the exhaust pull up into the cockpit. The suction caused by a wide transom will naturally draw these fumes forward. Under particular wind conditions they will blow off astern and be unnoticed.

The engine room has become a forgotten space. With the fine engines that are being produced these days it is a natural thing. However, I've seen some mighty small engine rooms, batteries almost impossible to remove, oil filler pipes unaccessable, working space at a minimum, and otherwise entirely impractical layouts. There is no sense in *asking* for such difficult conditions. For, with a little planning, an engine room can be safe, convenient and easy to use, as it should be.

The dual control, flying bridge design, No. 2, is a handsome looking boat. She will be easy to handle and a great pleasure to use.

Her original cost will be somewhat higher than the trunk cabin model. The dual controls alone will run some extra. They will be of great value in many ways and will be worth the extra cost. Handling the boat from the flying bridge is ideal on clear summer days. On days of inclement weather handling the boat from the main cabin will be

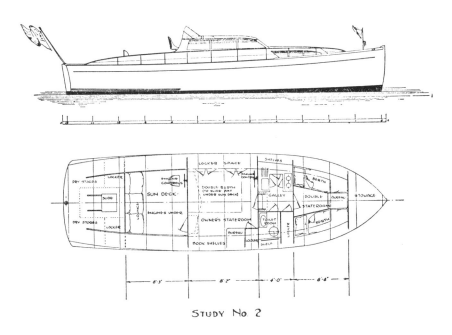

STUDY No. 2

HERE WE HAVE A SUN DECK-SEDAN TYPE DECK ARRANGEMENT FOR THE 36 FT. W.L. POWER CRUISER COMBINED WITH A LOW TRUNK CABIN FORWARD. THIS ARRANGEMENT PERMITS TWO STEERING WHEELS; ONE IN THE COCKPIT, THE OTHER IN THE SEDAN DECK HOUSE. THE DECK HOUSE ALSO SERVES AS THE OWNER'S STATEROOM.

most practical. With the full vision afforded by the flying bridge controls and the convenience of the interior ones they are well worth considering.

On this model to start forward we have suitable stowage space for tackle. The same deck space as shown for the other two designs provides footroom for handling mooring lines and anchors. Below we have a double cabin with full berths, stowage under these and a single bureau.

The galley, to port, is equipped with its necessary units, ice box, sink, stove, etc., and shelves for the galley stores. Ventilation is to be provided through the after window of the trunk cabin with standard electrical ventilation to carry away fumes from the stove top. This is a compact galley and in a position from which to hand food easily out to the main cabin; 6 ft. 3 in. headroom, combined with ample floor area will provide an ideal working space. The floor is to be covered with non-skid deck matting similar to Johnson's Biltright Mat.

A large hanging locker directly opposite the galley, with toilet room to starboard, is a convenient arrangement. A shower stall might be provided if desired.

The main cabin is light and airy. Engine controls and wheel are forward on the port side. A table, wicker chairs, etc. with the built-in bureau, lockers and book cases make up its normal furnishings. For sleeping purposes there is a large standard double bed which will slide out from the compartment over the engine room and below the sun deck. The owner requested a berth of such dimensions and we devised the arrangement shown. It is impractical in the sense of wasted space. Suitable casters will be provided so that the berth will be sea fixed both when in use and when stowed. A double berth, in a boat of this size, presents a problem. A studio couch type could be installed with the back forming one half of the made up berth. These, like all seats, have a tendency to be uncomfortable for sleeping and are difficult to make up. With the underside of the engine room deck well insulated I do not believe there will be trouble from heat.

The sun deck, with its controls, will be a perfectly lovely place to be in the boat in all weather. Motion will be slight and it is well protected from spray. The lounge, located as it is, will be far enough forward of the transom so that exhaust fumes will not be noticed and vision will be much better than from a lounge seat close to the transom.

Abaft the sun deck there is a sliding hatch with stowage space under it for all supplies, gear, etc. necessary for long cruises. Galley stores may be kept in two of the lockers and three or four days' supplies taken forward as required.

A dinghy can be stowed, bottom side up, on the deck over the dry stores compartment.

Suitable space is provided for a practical engine installation, tanks and other machinery. This compartment will be ventilated by standard electrical ventilation and natural air.

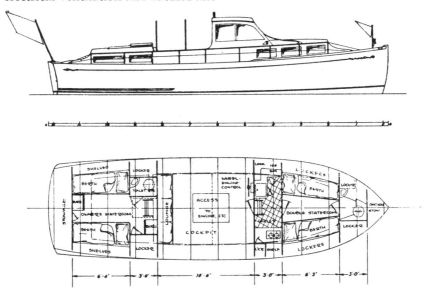

STUDY No. 3

THE DOUBLE CABIN MODEL IS IDEAL FOR TWO COUPLES. NOTICE THE DOUBLE STATEROOMS, EACH HAVING ITS OWN TOILET ROOM. THE COCKPIT HALF COVERED WITH PERMANENT TOP, HALF WITH CANVAS COVER, PROVIDES AN IDEAL OUTDOOR PLACE TO LIVE. FOR USE IN CROWDED WATERS THE STEERING LOCATION OF STUDY NO. 3 IS IN THE BEST POSSIBLE PLACE; WELL FORWARD AND GIVING EXCELLENT VISION AHEAD. LIKE THE OTHER STUDIES, THE SIDE DECKS ARE PROTECTED BY HAND RAILINGS.

Again the forward compartment is used for ground tackle. This space is possibly a little small but with a proper fore and aft division it will work out well.

In the double cabin model, study No. 3, we approach the perfect arrangement for the utmost in privacy and utility for a party of four in a boat this size.

Abaft the rope locker is a private toilet room for the forward double stateroom. Lockers are provided in the handiest place for keeping towels and other toilet articles. The w.c. is off the center line and will be easy to clean and quite accessible.

Two full berths in the stateroom to port and starboard, with lockers under and behind them, complete this compartment.

As in the trunk cabin model we have a galley the full width of the boat placed to accommodate the living space of the boat. Ventilation from windows and the hatchway will be ample. Ample room for full equipment is provided without cramming.

The main cockpit amidship has the advantages of the flying bridge study. One particular feature of this boat is the excellent vision which is afforded by placing the wheel and controls well forward and high. Coming up to docks, lock sides, moorings, etc. will be a much easier job with the controls so placed. A canvas shelter-top fitted over the pipe stanchions will make a snug spot in bad weather. The lounge across the after end of the cockpit will be a splendid, comfortable place to sit.

Complete quarters abaft the cockpit, combined with complete quarters forward, assure privacy and convenient cruising for two couples. A large hanging locker and bureau are on the starboard hand with toilet room to port. Abaft this are two full length berths and separate bureau. A small opening provides access to stowage space.

Among other advantages this arrangement provides privacy not found in the other studies. A person could be soundly sleeping forward or aft without there being any need of his being awakened by fellow crew members passing through the compartment; the steering position, as I previously mentioned, is well placed; a comfortable cockpit is amidship where it should be; her engine compartment is amidship, full and well planned; all in all she will be particularly handy to live aboard and to use.

As in the other two studies the engine room boasts of headroom and width not generally found on cruisers of her dimensions. Standard electrical ventilation, combined with natural, will keep the engine room free from fumes.

So there, Shipmates, as my father says, are three entirely practical studies in arranging a 37 foot hull for a particular need, family or prospective use. There are, quite naturally, many, many other ways in which this hull can be laid out.

It is our opinion that the double cabin model is best suited for the particular requirements given to us by the owner.

Perhaps you will find enjoyment in studying these three designs and seeing what developments and changes you would incorporate for your "dream ship." It is an interesting pastime and you will be amazed at the varied layouts possible in such a hull.

An auxiliary cruising sloop

Designed by Nelson Zimmer

O N the accompanying pages are the lines arrangement and sail plan of a little sloop designed by Mr. Nelson Zimmer who is associated with Mr. John Hacker, naval architect, of Detroit, Michigan. The plans show a boat 26 ft. 7 in. overall with a load water line of 18 ft. 9 in. Her beam is 7 ft. 11¼ in. and draft 4 ft. 5½ in.

Mr. Zimmer has produced a hull form which will be easy to drive and still be a comfortable boat in heavy weather. Consideration of the interior arrangement was not allowed to influence the hull form unduly. However the accommodations are well laid out and all that one might expect in a hull of but 18 ft. 9 in. on the water.

Ample space for ground tackle, extra line, etc. is provided in the eyes of the little boat. Abaft which are two full-sized berths with stowage space under each. Two shelves, to port and starboard above the berths, give additional space for stowing small articles.

When not in use the toilet is closed off from the rest of the cabin by a door which, when swung ninety degrees, separates the forward quarters from the rest of the cabin. There are shelves provided for linen and other necessities in the toilet room.

A large hanging locker, to starboard, is suitable for accommodating the personal gear of the crew. It is 1 ft. 9 in. long and allows full length hanging of clothes.

There is a comfortable place to sit in the main part of the cabin just forward of the galley range—a good spot to warm up in cold or wet weather.

The galley is also on the port side and well equipped. The ice box has 5 cu. ft. of stowage space with additional space for 200 lbs. of ice. Ice is loaded through a flush hatch on the bridge deck and eliminates the difficulties of carrying ice below.

Coal is passed to a bunker beneath the Shipmate range through a large deck plate fitted with a closed chute. This prevents dust and dirt from spreading around the cabin and is a practical idea.

To starboard there is a combination berth and settee. Outboard of

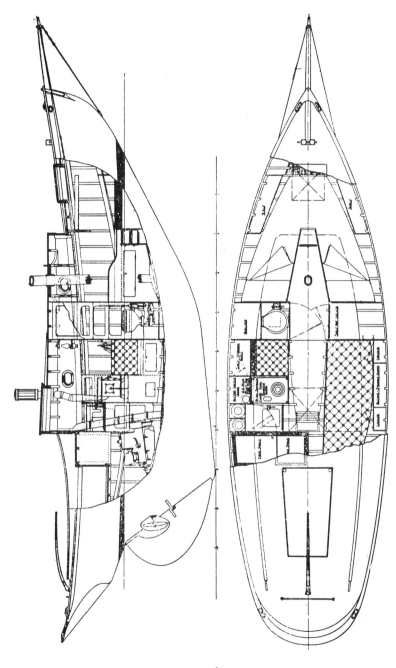

THE ARRANGEMENT SHOWN PROVIDES A SNUG MAIN CABIN, INCLUDING NICE SEATING SPACE AND THE GALLEY, WITH COMFORTABLE SLEEPING ACCOMMODATIONS FOR TWO OR THREE.

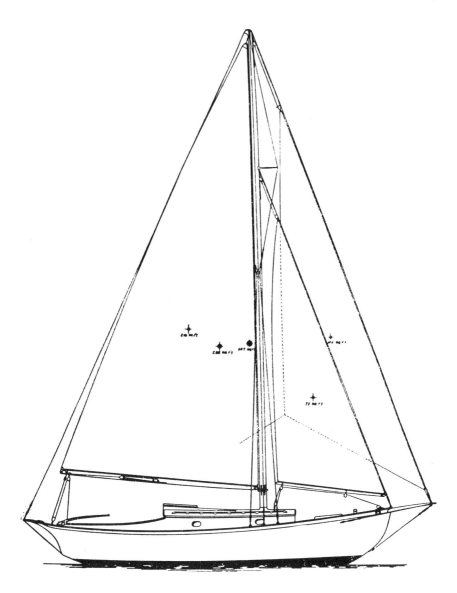

MR. ZIMMER'S AUXILIARY CRUISING SLOOP HAS A RIG WHICH IS SIMPLE
AND EFFICIENT. HER SAIL AREA TOTALS 288 SQ. FT. WITH 216 SQ. FT.
IN THE MAIN AND 72 SQ. FT. IN THE STAYSAIL. THE BOOM WILL CLEAR
THE BACKSTAY WHEN JIBING—AN IMPORTANT FACTOR SOMETIMES
OVER-LOOKED.

50

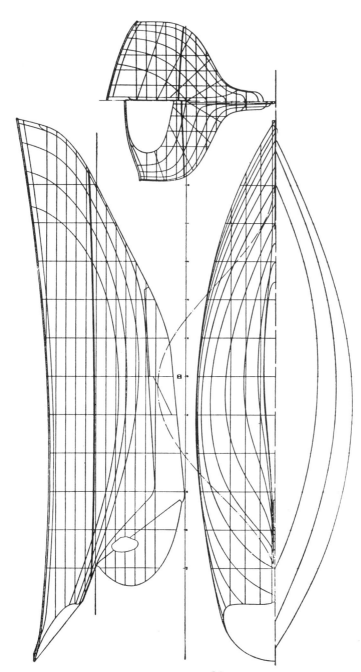

AS DRAWN THE LINES SHOULD PRODUCE A WHOLESOME SMALL CRUISING BOAT. THE CONTOUR OF THE STEM IS ESPECIALLY PLEASING. HER BODY PLAN SHOWS STRONG BILGES WHICH ARE AN INDICATION OF STIFFNESS.

51

this there is space for books, navigating instruments and odds and ends.

There is 6 ft. headroom under the companionway slide and 5 ft. 7 in. under the cabin carlins.

The engine shown is a two cylinder Universal Fisherman. Fuel and water tanks, located to port and starboard under the cockpit, have a combined capacity of 70 gals.

The rig, as shown, is simple and practical. The permanent backstay is designed to clear the end of the boom regardless of how high the latter may rise up in jibing. This is a very important factor often overlooked in many such rigs. A large genoa jib and parachute spinnaker may be carried to advantage in light weather. There is a total of 397 sq. ft. of area in the three sails, with 288 sq. ft. in the working sails and 109 additional sq. ft. with the jib set.

The boat has a displacement of 7,600 lbs. and carries 2,800 lbs of lead on the keel.

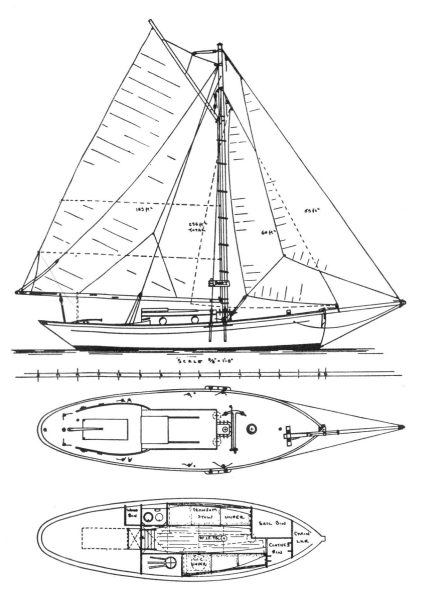

Dart IS MR. FUNK'S "DREAM SHIP." PERHAPS SOMEDAY SOON TO BE-
COME A REALITY. SHE IS WHOLESOME AND EXTREMELY PRACTICAL. AC-
COMMODATIONS INCLUDE COMPLETE FACILITIES FOR ONE—A SINGLE
HANDER.

Dart

Designed by J. B. Funk, Jr.

HERE is the sail plan and arrangements of a single hander ᶜ
by Mr. J. B. Funk, Jr., who is now operating the Boat
Westport, Conn. Possibly inspired by Mr. Kunhardt's ar
titled A DEFINITION, which appears on pages 21 to 26 of th
and prompted by the desire to design a little boat for his own
pleasant to see Mr. Funk's resulting *Dart*, an able and attracti
ton cutter.

Mr. Zimmer arranged the interior of his sloop to conform
lines and not unduly affect the arrangement. In contrast to t
Funk has arranged the interior of *Dart* to suit his requirements ɑ
developed lines of a character suitable to accommodate these. I(
or less a compromise which all designers must face.

In both cases, the results are favorable—depending entire
a prospective owner's desires.

The lines of *Dart* show a well-proportioned hull. Unfor
these were not available for reproduction at the time of publiᶜ

Mr. Funk shows a sail plan which will be easy to use. Sh
sail in good proportion is possible, still maintaining trim and ɑ
reach and go to windward under varying weather conditions. T
sail has 183 sq. ft. of area and is made to take two deep reef;
with lazyjacks, no trouble will be experienced with the sail
away from the spars or off the deck when lowering in a bre(
staysail contains 60 sq. ft. and the jib, 53 sq. ft. These total(
her sail area to 296 sq. ft., which is a comfortable amount o[
this kind of boat. A reaching jib is also shown and could b(
advantage.

Runners are shown and these will only be used in pa
windy weather. Close reaching or on the wind the leach of the
forms a preventer. Therefore, all the haste and rushing abou
up and respectively releasing windward and leeward runners
essary excepting when sheets are eased. Under normal sailir
tions the runners may be led forward and made fast to the sh(
Handy to use when required and entirely out of the way whe[

Dart's deck is well arranged for single handed work and

paratively low and narrow trunk becomes the rest of the hull. A dead-light on the foredeck provides light in the forecastle.

A wide companionway opens up the after end of the trunk cabin. Flaring coamings and a narrow well provide comfortable space for sitting. The cockpit is self bailing.

Starting forward below decks in *Dart* we find a locker for general ground tackle. Abaft this, to port, a sail bin, which will accommodate the staysail, jib and reaching jib—the mainsail will remain on the spars. Opposite this bin, there is a clothes locker, which is designed to take duffle bags and such, though not to provide for immaculate and un-wrinkled storage of suits and topcoats.

To port and starboard, slightly staggered, there are two seats. A transom berth forms the back of the seat on the port hand. An arrange-ment, such as this, allows the seats to be narrow enough for complete sitting comfort and a berth solely for sleeping.

A drop leaf table is fitted between the two seats. Under the aft end of the starboard berth Mr. Funk has indicated a water closet. While there are many pros and cons on the subject of installing water closets in small single handers it must be admitted a certain amount of comfort is maintained with one. One's wife may be a hearty "shipmate" but modern living has caused all of us to desire as many comforts as possi-ble. There is not much sense in spending time aboard a boat in total discomfort.

At the after end of the cabin a galley is indicated—Shipmate to port, with wood bin, and sink and counter-top to port—with stowage space provided under the sink. There is 5 ft. 4 in. headroom under the cabin top, and about 4 in. more beneath the companionway slide. When the slide is open there will be ample ventilation provided while cooking.

Dart is 21 ft. 6 in. on deck and 18 ft. 0 in. on the water line. Her moderate beam of 6 ft. 0 in. and draft of 3 ft. 3 in. are in excellent proportion.

Idler II

Abel Brown

I POKED about Dick Hartge's yard at Galesville on the West River in the Chesapeake country of Maryland, and found there a 42 ft. ketch, *Idler II,* which Dick had just launched after designing and building for Mr. C. Earle Kline of Washington, D. C. I liked the little ship.

Dick Hartge was fashioning a deck cleat of seasoned yellow locust, from a tree which he had cut down from his back yard. This will look a lot better than a metal one, on a sailboat anyway.

The cabin carlins were shaped and built up; boards about 5/16 in. thick and 5 in. wide were cold bent over a form and glued one atop the other. When set, they were sawed lengthwise, giving 4 carlins 7/8 in. wide and 2 in. deep; immensely strong and also economical of good lumber.

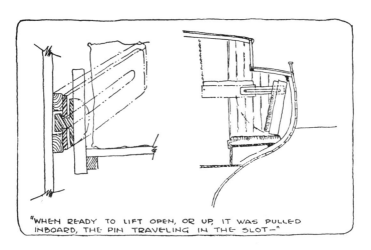

"WHEN READY TO LIFT OPEN, OR UP, IT WAS PULLED INBOARD, THE PIN TRAVELING IN THE SLOT—"

The upper bunks fold down to form the backs of the lowers. The hinging pin at the ends of each upper bunk frame is set in a horizontally slotted brass strip very much like a hatch slide slot. When the bunk is down it may be pushed back under the deck; when ready to lift open,

56

or up, it is pulled inboard, the pin traveling in the slot and thus bringing the bunk inboard and free of the deck overhang.

The main traveler is set atop a wooden frame which looks like another huge traveler and this lower frame is set atop the cabin but clears

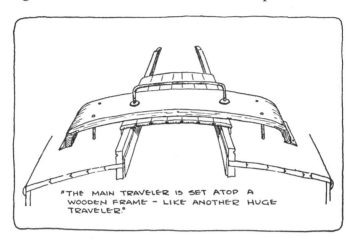

"THE MAIN TRAVELER IS SET ATOP A WOODEN FRAME – LIKE ANOTHER HUGE TRAVELER."

the main cabin hatch, by an inch or so, when the hatch is open. The mainsheet thus never interferes with the main hatchway.

There is a swinging stirrup which acts as the main boom crotch hinged on the forward side of the jigger mast; this stirrup swings forward and into it is hooked the after end of the main boom.

The jigger boom crotch is the same shape and nearly as long as the boomkin; the latter a fine strong flat one. The crotch is hinged at the boomkin's butt. When it is swung up it acts as a crotch; when swung down it is out of the way. The crotch lays against the boomkin and makes a wide, stable footing for the lad who has to work a reef in the jigger.

Both crotching devices are not only simple but handy. They could have been badly made and still been 100 per cent better than the old scissor type which has caused more head and hand injuries than any other device used afloat.

A neighbor to *Idler II* is the cutter *Lorna,* owned by Mr. F. H. Russell of Bucks County, Pennsylvania. One of those wonderful little ships of a previous generation. She was built in 1895. Will the yachts built today be still afloat in the year 2000? The well built ones may; those built in haste for handsome figures will not. For a large part of

57

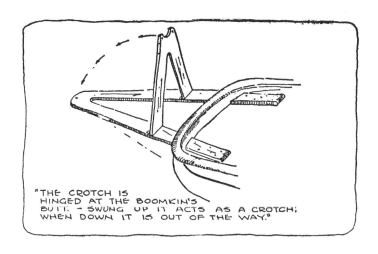

"THE CROTCH IS HINGED AT THE BOOMKIN'S BUTT. — SWUNG UP IT ACTS AS A CROTCH; WHEN DOWN IT IS OUT OF THE WAY."

her life little *Lorna* depended upon wind alone. Skippers in those days were patient seamen; they generally waited out another tide rather than slide in over oyster banks, rocks, and hard bottoms in order to get home "in time". Dick Hartge's slant is that there were plenty of experienced, careful boat-loving hands around a yard in older days, to check up on a sagged winter cover, an out of place shoring beam, a moored boat bumping her bottom at dead low tide and other incidents which tend to shorten the life of a boat.

Lorna was built by an old master mariner who planned to take her around the world. He died all too soon; then the late Mr. Starling Burgess bought her. Mr. Russell has had the boat for about the last ten years.

This little ship is about as old as I am, but probably a lot sounder. Boats get creaky and soft but unlike humans they don't get stiff joints in their old age.

Facts about rope

*Frederick K. Lord**

M ANILA rope is made of wild banana fibre from the Philippines. Hemp rope is from the hemp plant. Russian hemp is most used for cordage and Italian for packing. New Manila and hemp ropes are of about equal strength, but the latter does not stand the weather so well and is seldom used on ships, except as tarred standing rigging, as it is not pliable enough. Coir rope, from cocoanut husk, is used for tow lines. It is lighter, and does not become water logged, but is not so strong.

Tarring prolongs life, but weakens the rope, especially hemp, about 25 per cent. Ropes should not be laid away wet, as they rapidly deteriorate. Four strand ropes are about 15 per cent stronger than three; but, in hawsers and cables, four strands are 10 per cent weaker than three. Hawsers and cables have 40 per cent less strength than good Manila rope. The strength of the latter is about 16,000 pounds per square inch.

Rope has no "elastic limit". Under excessive strain the fibres begin to slip by one another and the rope ultimately breaks. Hence, excessive loads tend to weaken it. Splicing reduces its strength about 15 per cent.

WEIGHT AND STRENGTH OF MANILA ROPE

Diam.	Breaking Strain Best	Good	Ft. Per Lb.	Diam.	Breaking Strain Best	Good	Ft. Per Lb.
1/4	610	590	60	1 3/16	5600	4900	5.1
5/16	1000	800	40	7/8	6500	5800	4.4
3/8	1300	1000	29	1	7700	7400	3.5
7/16	1900	1400	20	1 1/8	10200	9700	2.6
1/2	2300	1800	14	1 1/4	12700	12200	2.3
9/16	3100	2500	10	1 3/8	14100	13500	1.7
5/8	3700	3000	8	1 1/2	17000	16200	1.5
3/4	4900	4000	6	2	30000	29000	.84

The working load should not exceed one fifth the breaking strain.

*From the rare little book,
HANDY DATA FOR THE YACHTING WORLD

Shore Liner, a development of Black Skimmer

Ed Hanks

WITH these sketches and ideas, I've been guided by the results of experience during five years or so with *Black Skimmer*. The things that proved useful have been retained; otherwise the present boat is larger with more accommodation, fairer lines and an even simpler rig.

Like *Black Skimmer* she is flat-bottomed. Deadrise aft would clear her quarters, but would get away from simplicity. Not worth it. Same reason no attempt toward prettying up the bow—plumb stem pretty enough. Flat keel or shoe—skeg running aft, at no point deeper than the draft amidships.

For strength and space below, the deckhouse extends to the sides; moderate camber to deckhouse beams, otherwise the footing will be un-handy, uncertain—dangerous. Seems possible to obtain close to 48 in. headroom in the clear within the cabin; about 36 in. under the forward deck. Would permit two persons to sleep on mattresses right on the floorboards forward. Cabin berths can be raised as high as practicable for sitting headroom.

Cabin doors, full length, open into the cockpit; floorboards continue right on out from the cabin for the length of the cockpit. Should be a sill with a 2 in. stop. Doors have square-hinged wooden shutters—very useful when it rains. Going in or out of this cabin requires no gymnastics.

Cockpit is deep, fairly narrow, only for leg and foot room. The deck is the cockpit seat—and is long enough to stretch out full length. Clear hot nights, can bring mattresses out here. Good stowage space under deck each side, should be closed in and fitted with removable doors (battens and thumb-catch). Have shown a caulked deck—canvas more practical. *Black Skimmer* had deck fill-caps set in deck either side just abaft house, covering vertical brass pipes leading to bilge. Pump piston with valve (fitting pipe diameter) on shaft with T handle provided practical pump arrangement.

Forward deck broken by hatch with smoothly rounded corners—no place for gear to hang up. For ventilation and access to forecastle

60

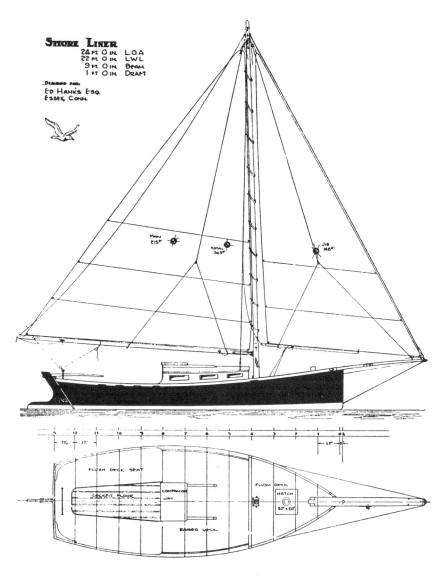

SHORE LINER

24 ft 0 in LOA
22 ft 0 in LWL
9 ft 0 in BEAM
1 ft 0 in DRAFT

Designed for
ED HANKS ESQ.
ESSEX, CONN.

MAIN
215⁰

TOTAL
365⁰

JIB
145⁰

FLUSH DECK SEAT

COCKPIT FLOOR

COMPANION WAY

RAISED DECK

FLUSH DECK HATCH
20" x 20"

EXPERIENCE IN *Black Skimmer* PROVED THAT REEFING WAS A COMMON OCCURRENCE. JIB WILL TAKE TWO REEFS—THE MAIN, THREE. GOOD DEEP ONES.—THE DECK IS THE COCKPIT SEAT AND IS LONG ENOUGH TO STRETCH OUT FULL LENGTH.

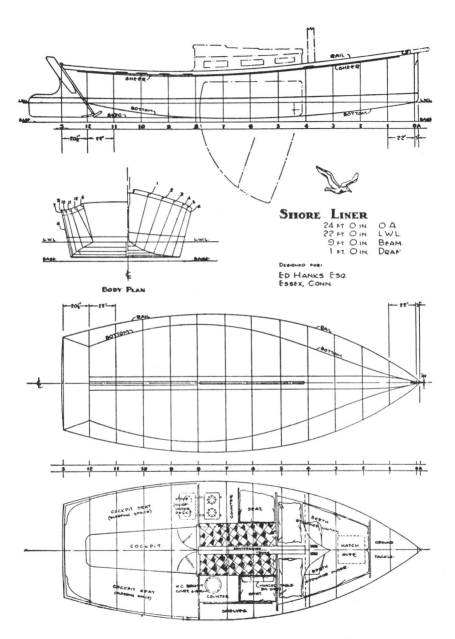

SHORE LINER

24 FT 0 IN. O A
22 FT 0 IN. LWL.
9 FT 0 IN. BEAM
1 FT 0 IN. DRAFT

DESIGNED FOR:
ED HANKS ESQ.
ESSEX, CONN.

BODY PLAN

THE LINES AND ARRANGEMENT OF MR. HANK'S *Shore Liner.*

berths. Bulkhead between forward and main berths up to you. Would provide great strength in way of shrouds and support for center-board case. Would make forecastle damned stuffy on a rainy night. Perhaps a partial bulkhead for structural strength—a detail.

Shoal-draft cruisers such as this little boat have one cruising advantage over deep draft boats—the ability to negotiate interesting (and snug and safe) small creeks and coves and holes. This advantage she should be able to use to the full extent. Too often small creeks are limited to navigation by low-fixed bridges. Hence, the hinged mast in the tabernacle. To my mind this has more good features than bad. Common usage in North Europe, England. So she has a pole mast, jibstay, pair of shrouds, boom topping lift.

As drawn, the center of effort may be criticized for undue lead. *Black Skimmer* had a rugged center-board customarily carried hanging all the way down, moving her center lateral resistance forward. Different ships, different long-splices. But whether or not the bowsprit is shortened, its upper surface should be flat for safer footing. (Incidentally, it has always been my idea that a hull of this kind needs a long rather than a tall rig.)

Jib fitted with club with sheet rigged as shown. Both ends of jib sheet lead aft to cleats near quarters; trimming always accomplished on weather side. Club is slightly shorter than second line of reef-points.

My opinion, jib should be made to take two reefs—the main, three. Good deep ones. Experience in *Black Skimmer* proved that reefing was a common occurrence. There will be occasions when it is necessary to beat in against plenty of breeze; the sail-plan should be balanced for sailing close-reefed. Initial stability will bring this type back only from a limited angle of heel, and in a boat this size three or four adults on the weather rail have little effect. Better be prepared to keep moving with sails filled than to kill headway luffing with too much sail on her. A harder puff—knockdown—capsize. It is my considered belief that this is one of the most necessary subjects for including in her plans.

Other than bunks—settees—no definite suggestions for use of space at after end of cabin. All sorts of arrangements possible, as certain equipment can be fitted to slide in and out of the spaces under the after deck. Depending on the nature of the owner, there is space for an icebox, two-burner stove, straight through toilet (?) (at least a good solid thunder mug), dishpan, etc.

Do not believe in cluttering up this boat with an inboard engine. Outboard, if locality (such as Essex, Conn.) demands one. Good stowage space for engine under either side of after decks. *Black Skimmer* had a three inch bulwark with a cap-rail (so has this one). On the port side of the taffrail two rowlock sockets were let in. Into these sockets, when required, fitted two galvanized iron thole pins. A long sculling oar was introduced between these and provided motive power. Poling in shoal water, use of the spinnaker pole on one side and the oar on the other kept two people healthfully employed and developed a speed of knots.

Mention of spinnaker reminds me: With this boat, a sail used alternately as genoa and spinnaker is possible. With forethought it can be a spare mainsail!

Black Skimmer had obvious faults—her sheer forward was too abrupt. And yet she had a certain character, a quality that was appealing; she wasn't just another little sailboat—she was a cocky little hooker. You know what I mean.

* * *

Guided by Mr. Ed Hanks requirements and preliminary sketches, Atkin & Co. of Darien, Conn., prepared the design of *Shore Liner*. The result is an extremely practical, inexpensive cruising boat.

The designers managed to maintain the 48 in. clear headroom in the cabin. The interior arrangement goes into a little more detail than Mr. Hanks specified. As he said, the arrangement may be altered, to suit the owner, with consideration given to weight distribution.

Shore Liner is arranged to accommodate two comfortably. The double berth forward is 6 ft. 3 in. long. The hatch in the fore deck provides ventilation and emergency escape.

To port and starboard, abaft the berth, are upholstered, single seats, places just "to sit", usually not found in the cabin of small cruising boats. These, with a table hinged on the centerboard trunk, provide comfortable furnishings for eating, reading, and a place as well on which to spread charts.

Stowage space is provided under the berths, under the cockpit seats and in the lockers behind the counter and starboard seat. The after end of the cuddy contains the galley, with a Primus stove (fitted on sail track so as to slide under the cockpit deck when not in use) on the port side and a counter top opposite. A water closet, in the form of an enameled bucket, is fitted under this counter.

The cockpit seats are flush with the deck. They may be used for sleeping during particularly warm weather. The cockpit floor continues out from the main cabin, with a high sill designed to prevent water from entering the cabin.

The deck arrangement is practicable and simple and it will be noticed nothing protrudes to catch sheets and other rigging. The raised sides and deck amidships add to the room below, and with its tumble home this arrangement is well adapted to the design.

The sail plan is the utmost in simplicity with a total area of 365 sq. ft. distributed in mainsail, 215 sq. ft. and the staysail 148 sq. ft. Deep reefs are

THE PROTOTYPE *Black Skimmer* UNDER SAIL IN A LIGHT BREEZE. SHE HAS A PARTICULAR CHARM WHICH IS DIFFICULT TO DEFINE BUT EASY TO SEE.

shown, as requested by Mr. Hanks. These will prove their worth many times over. Lazy jacks are fitted to both main and staysail. The mast is set in a tabernackle to enable the owner to lower away to explore shallow creeks and streams which are likely to be bridged over at many places.

And so the designers hope *Shore Liner* as shown here, will come close to suiting her owner's requirements and trust that, as Mr. Hanks said of *Black Skimmer,* "She has a certain character, a quality that is appealing; she isn't just another sailboat—she is a cocky little hooker. You know what I mean."

Nebula

A reproduction of an etching by

Mr. Cornelius W. Van Ness

Nebula

The oldest yacht listed
in Lloyd's Register of American Yachts

NEBULA was designed and built in 1885 by George Lawley & Son at South Boston, Mass. She is one of the very old "genuine" cutters now afloat on the east coast. *Nebula*, like *Petrel*, is an example of character and charm combined with the very important features of being "sea-kindly", practical and wholesome. No sailing on "one ear" in *Nebula*.

Her rig, old fashioned as it may be in appearance, with deadeyes and lanyards, mast hoops, topmast and gaff main sail, has stood the test of time. And has proven far less expensive and easier to maintain than the rigs of her modern counterparts.

While some may say, "she is a workhouse", others can answer, "perhaps men were stronger in the days they built such able boats. Perhaps their backs were a little broader, a little more willing to bend to a task".

Whatever the answer may be, it is quite evident that *Nebula* has simplicity. There are few "gadgets and gillhickies", two senseless words at best, to contend with, few indeed. Mr. Edward "Mump" Sturgis, of Westport, Conn., owned and sailed *Nebula* for some time and was truly appreciative of all her good qualities.

Constructed in the finest manner, her frame is of white oak, her planking, of long leaf yellow pine and her deck, white pine. All of her brightwork is mahogany and, while showing signs of age, it is evident that the original materials and workmanship were first class.

Nebula is described in Lloyd's Register of American Yachts as a flush deck, auxiliary cutter of 16 gross tons. She has an overall length of 44 ft. 6 in. and is 36 ft. long on the water line, with a breadth of 12 ft. 3 in., and a draft of 7 ft. 10 in.

Mr. Clarence S. Jones was the original owner and since his ownership *Nebula* has been in the hands of many famous yachtsmen.

Mr. J. William Ellsworth is the present owner and she has, as her port of call, Greenport, L. I., N. Y.

Mr. Cleat

Gay Mary

Pocket Cruiser from England

Gay Mary GIVES THE
IMPRESSION OF BE-
ING MUCH BIGGER
THAN SHE IS.

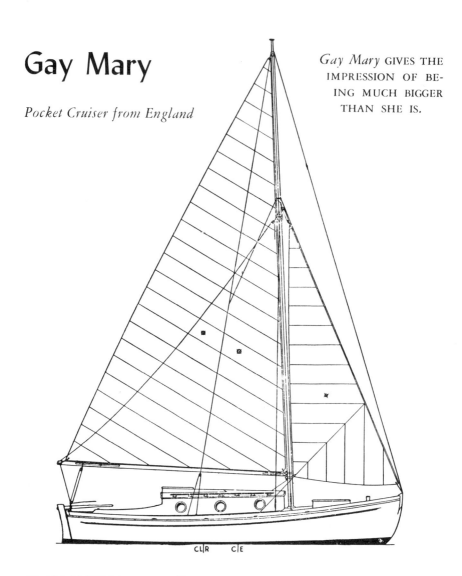

CL|R   C|E

G AY MARY is an auxiliary cruising yacht 18 ft., 0 in. o.a., 16 ft.,
10 in. w.l., the beam being 6 ft., 6 in. and draught 3 ft., 4 in.

She has a pleasing appearance and the underwater form is carefully balanced, with the result that she handles nicely under sail.

According to the editor of England's YACHTING WORLD, who
carefully examined the plans and sailed the completed boat—"When

examining her lines we came across a few points, none of them very serious, which seem to call for comment. It must be remembered that the smaller the vessel the more difficult are the problems which beset her creator. Messrs. Brooke's chief designer is to be congratulated upon having produced such an able little vessel which will be a joy to own and a pleasure to sail.

"The midship section is inclined to be easy in the bilge and would be more appropriate to a bigger hull, since although she has a fair amount of beam, she could be made a little stiffer. The load water line is very full forward with a slight shoulder near section 3, but it tails off with rather a weak after ending. A certain lack of harmony is apparent between bow and stern and the buttocks aft do not show as clean a run as they might. Distribution of weights is an important factor in a small boat. In this case the center of gravity of the iron keel almost coincides with the fore-and-aft position of the center of buoyancy and the weight of two people in the cockpit will put her down by the stern.

"Since much of her cruising may be done in narrow waters the deadwood forward might have been cut away a little more to increase speed and make her quicker in stays.

"It is something of an achievement to have managed to squeeze two berths, galley, oilskin locker, w.c. and an auxiliary motor into a hull only 18 ft. long. All the necessities for cruising have been provided. The height from the cabin sole to the coachroof beams is 4 ft., 2 in., and there is nearly 3 ft. of sitting headroom. It is especially pleasing to see an oilskin locker for it is so often omitted in small cruisers, and the smaller the ship the more it is necessary. The provision of a sink in the galley, however, is more questionable. There seems no reason why the bunk on the starboard side should not have been made a few inches longer than 6 ft. so that a tall member of the crew could unbend.

"A 4 h.p. Stuart Turner engine stows neatly under the cockpit and is of sufficient power."

Scantlings follow good boat building practice and include an oak stem, sided 5 in. English elm keel, sided 4 in. and sternknee of oak sided 2 in. The transom is English elm 1½ in. thick with floor timbers of iron 1½ in by ½ in. tapered as required. Frames are rock elm 1¾ in. by ¾ in. and planking ⅝ in. pine. Main deck beams are 2 in. by 2 in. oak with cabin top beams 1¾ in. square. Cabin top is tongue and groove ½ in. pine canvas covered.

69

THE SMALLER THE VESSEL THE MORE DIFFICULT ARE PROBLEMS WHICH BESET HER CREATOR. "PICK" BROOKE, HER DESIGNER, IS TO BE CONGRATULATED UPON HAVING PRODUCED SUCH A LITTLE VESSEL.

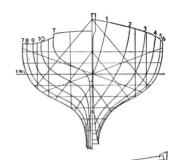

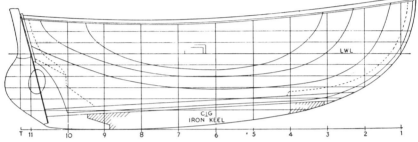

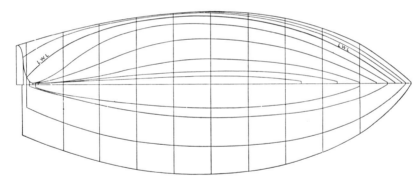

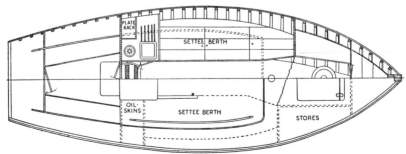

Rigged as a Bermudian Sloop this little 2½ tonner has a mainsail of 124 sq. ft. and a jib of 71 sq. ft. Standing rigging is of galvanized plough steel wire and all running rigging of yacht Manila.

Several of these interesting little boats have been produced by Brooke Marine Ltd., Oulton Broad, Lowestoft, England.

Gay Mary ON OULTON BROAD.
A BROOKE 2½ TONNER.

Powerboat of tomorrow-- designed in 1939

Photographs by Kaufmann & Fabry Co.

L ATE in the fall of 1938 Mr. Sam W. Robertson, of Minneapolis, Minn., wrote to us in connection with having designs made of a distinctive type of power boat and a few weeks later visited our office which at that time was on Pratt Island.

The outcome was his commissioning us to prepare plans for him. One of his primary requirements was to have this boat a small edition of famed *Q. E. D.*, the very modern 115 ft. cruiser then owned by the late Mr. Anthony Fokker. We had prepared all the preliminary drawings for *Q. E. D.* and therefore were in a position to prepare a smaller version similar to it.

Mr. Robertson also wanted his boat to have the same "modern-

Alba R AS SHE APPEARED ABOUT ONE YEAR AFTER LAUNCHING.

THE LIVING QUARTERS ARE FINISHED IN WHITE PINE AND BAMBOO.

line" theme of the Lincoln-Zephyr automobile. He saw no reason for a power boat having a square stern, high standing top and other conventional features. We then obtained the balance of his requirements in the manner of accommodations, speed, performance expected, cruising radius and all the information needed in helping to prepare a successful design.

The yacht is 44 ft. 6 in. overall. A long clipper bow gives her overhang forward and her stern has considerable tumble home which gives a waterline length of 41 ft. Her breadth of 13 ft. is a little less than one-third her length. She draws 3 ft. of water at station 8, which is the deepest point.

Alba R was arranged to suit her owner's requirements and has worked out nicely. In the forepeak a locker extends the full width of the boat. Above this, just ahead of the trunk cabin, there is a forward cockpit. Such a cockpit makes an ideal place to sit, as it is quiet—the vision excellent. Abaft the locker is a private cabin with double berths on the port hand. An enclosed toilet room and dressing table are opposite. This cabin assures the privacy of guests and is complete in itself.

The galley, immediately forward of the deck house, is 6 ft. 2 in. long and also extends the full width of the boat. Sink, stove and refrigerator, with counter space and lockers are on the starboard side. Dining table and two seats, arranged as a dinette, are to port.

The deckhouse is the "living area" and is furnished in white pine and bamboo. As the accompanying photograph shows on page 81, the boat had all the comforts of home. A small piano was especially built to match the finish and theme of the cabin. An upholstered seat is fitted around the after corner of the deck house, to port. In the forward end of the deckhouse there is a distinctive bar also finished in bamboo.

The boat is presently powered with two 70 h. p. gasoline engines which give her a cruising speed of 14 miles an hour.

The owner's stateroom, aft, is another complete living unit, containing an enclosed toilet room on the port hand and a large hanging

THE OWNER'S QUARTERS ARE PLAINLY FINISHED IN EXCELLENT TASTE.

locker to starboard. Single berths on either side of the cabin, with a built in bureau between these, complete the arrangement. The after end of this cabin is shown in the photograph on this page.

John Atkin.

Store of information

Conducted by the
Messrs. Cleat, Garboard and Ratline

W E have gathered together, from our own experiences, from the experiences of valued cruising friends, and from many other reliable sources, a group of recipes, procedures, rudiments, instruction and intelligent understandings, that should be of great value to our Shipmates.

We intend to continue this STORE OF INFORMATION in future issues and will be very glad to receive contributions of this character from readers.

Among questions we've received from members of the yachting fraternity are—how to prevent mildew—methods of preventing iron ballast from rusting—how to bleach white oak—and all manner of problems to which it is so difficult to find satisfactory and reliable answers.

And so to start we have a question asked by many sailing men— what is a satisfactory method of preventing mildew?

It may be prevented, to a great degree, by soaking the canvas in the following preparation: dissolve 3 lbs. of sugar of lead in 15 gals. of fresh water. In another tub mix 4 lbs. of finely powdered alum in a similar quantity of fresh water. The two liquids are then poured into a large, clean tank—an old enameled bath tub is satisfactory—stirred well and the sails (or canvas) completely immersed. Push the sails well down into the mixture with a smooth, round stick. Be certain that they are completely covered. After pickling for 24 hours, the sails should be removed and hung to dry under an open shed. At Greenport, L. I., it is the practice to lay the sails out on the clean beach. However, hanging the sails under a shed is more satisfactory as it allows the mixture to drain off and the sails to dry gradually. Nothing will remove mildew so it is highly advisable to go through the above operation when the sails are first purchased.

Here are some facts about canvas that may be interesting. Canvas or duck is made from flax, hemp, and cotton. Yacht sails are normally made of cotton. Sails on commercial ships of an older day were made of flax. The word "duck" is understood to be cotton duck unless it is stated otherwise. Duck is manufactured in the following standard widths: 14, 16, 18, 20, 22, 24, and 30 inches. It is also made in "wide duck" up to 208 inches for using on cabin tops, decks of small boats, awnings, etc. Weights of duck run by numbers from No. 00, the heaviest, to No. 12, the lightest. Another series of very heavy canvas runs from No. 000 to Twelve 0. This is, however, not often used in connection with yachts.

There is still another series, more common among yachtsmen, and this is called U. S. Army Duck. Its weight is designated in ounces per yard, 28½ in. wide. There are six weights as follows: 7, 8, 9, 10, 12, and 15 ounces. Canvas is normally about 25 per cent stronger crossways than lengthwise, this is one of the reasons why the cloths in most present day sails extend crossways to their leaches.

Some old fashioned methods used to waterproof canvas consist of using 6 oz. of hard yellow soap dissolved in 1½ pts. of fresh water. When brought to a boiling point add 5 lbs. of ground ochre, ½ lb. of patent driers and 5 lbs. of boiled linseed oil. These quantities will want to be added to proportionately according to the size and quantity of canvas desired to be waterproofed. Another time proven formula is to obtain 1 quart of boiled linseed oil to which add 1 oz. of soap and 1 oz. of beeswax. Boil these together until reduced to the consistency of thick paint. Brush this well into the canvas and allow to dry in the sun for two or three days.

A satisfactory method of stopping checks and surface cracks in spars follows. This method should be followed closely and precautions taken to see that the mast is carefully scraped, sanded and cleaned before application is made. The spars should be in a horizontal position and preliminary study given to a practical method of slowly turning the spar so that the check is up to receive the liquid. Obtain the very best grade of linseed oil available. Heat 1 pt. of this linseed oil to about 150 degrees farenheit. When the oil reaches this temperature add 2 lbs. of pure white resin and 8 oz. of a good grade palm oil. Stir this mixture well until thoroughly mixed and then pour into the checks. The solution will harden and can be varnished or painted over without any difficulty.

For those of us who have forgotten grammar school arithmetic the following method of figuring the capacity of cylindrical tanks may come in handy: the capacity of a cylindrical tank in U. S. gallons = dia.² in inches X length in inches X .0034. Good, heavy rectangular copper gasoline tanks for motor boats will weigh approximately one pound per gallon, in moderate sizes. 231 cu. in. = 1 gal. 1 gal. water = 8.34 lbs. 1 gal. gasoline = 5.6 lbs.

Another question, often asked by members of the power boat group, is a satisfactory method of preparing stew. Not just the preparing of stew in an every day power boat—but a method that can be used aboard one of the more "brilliant planning hulls," while traveling at great speed over the turbulent waters.

For this recipe we called upon our old friend Abel Brown. He was the logical one to supply this.

Abel writes, "After a considerable amount of tinkering with various methods I have reached the conclusion that if you take a pot with a diameter of P and an overall height of H and fill it with $\pi \left(\frac{P}{2}\right)^2 H$ of stew, and you put it on a Shipmate range which is heeled to an angle θ, then $\pi \left(\frac{P}{2}\right)^2 \times \dfrac{P \tan \theta}{2}$ goes on the floor and you have only $\pi \left(\frac{P}{2}\right)^2 \times \left(H - \dfrac{P \tan \theta}{2}\right)$ of the stew left."

While Abel's method of preparing stew appears complicated it is actually a very simple matter in comparison with the formulae required in the preparation of a design for a theoretical "brilliant planning hull."

To take the place of Tally Ho!

William Atkin

THE good little cutter *Tally Ho!* changed owners two summers ago, my old friend "Newt." Wigton of Huntington, N. Y. having sold her to Mr. M. J. Kony of Great Neck, N. Y. *Tally Ho!* is a heavy displacement plumb stem and stern auxiliary designed after the manner of the excellent cruising yachts that are so popular in British yachting centers. For thirteen years *Tally Ho!* served the needs of her first owner so well that she was a little difficult to part with; a parting not unlike that of the moving of a loved one to some distant land. However what is Mr. Wigton's loss is Mr. Kony's gain, and while this has its comforting aspects it, never-the-less, left the original owner of *Tally Ho!* without a cruising boat. And a cruising man without a boat, or the prospects of having a boat, is a saddened man indeed.

Thus it comes about that I have drawn the third design for my shipmate "Newt" Wigton. And how different this is from the first two! A centerboard skipjack this time, one of those half-flat bottomed sailing boats that for generations have been plying the waters of Chesapeake Bay.

Fine boats these are and equally adapted for making ones living at clamming, crabbing, oystering, and fishing or, with a little dressing up, excellent boats to use for fun. To be sure there is not the full headroom one finds in deep keel boats, and this should not be expected; but in these there is the advantage of being able to poke into all manner of small harbors and creeks which are forbidden to yachts of generous draft. I can think of many of these places up and down Long Island Sound, along the Cape, and even all the way Down East; quiet little places undisturbed by deep sea-going racing yachts whose crews are prone to wear scarlet trousers and whose deportment is likely to be quite as loud as their gaudy breeches. Yes, there are many shallow harbors where peace caresses the water and where quiet drifts in on the wings of the wind. And, Shipmates, an excellent way to reach them is in a little boat like this latest one I have designed for the one time owner of the cutters, *Fore An' Aft* and *Tally Ho!*.

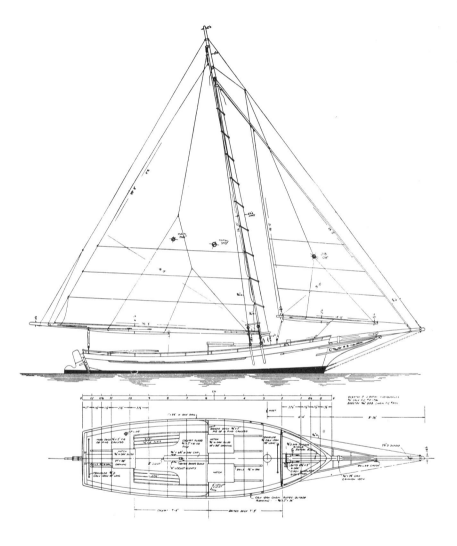

THE SAIL PLAN HAS ALL THE EAR-MARKS OF THE WORKING BOATS OF
THE CHESAPEAKE; THE TAPERING MAST, THE STEEP RAKE, THE LONG
BOW SPRIT, THE SIMPLICITY OF THE STANDING AND RUNNING RIGGING,
AND PLEASING BALANCE BETWEEN THE JIB AND MAINSAIL.

The plans of the skipjack show a boat that is typical of Chesapeake Bay. As drawn the over all length, excluding the billet-head is 24 ft. 6½ in.; the length on the water line is, 22 ft. 6 in.; the extreme breadth is, 7 ft. 6½ in.; and the draft with center board up, is 2 ft. 0½ in. The freeboard at the bow is, 3 ft. 4 in.; and at the stern, 1 ft. 11¼ in.; the freeboard being measured to the edge of the deck. The long graceful billet-head and trail boards, which are as much a part of this type boat as the keel, add another 4 ft. 10 in. to the over all length as given above. The lines show a big center board, this being 7 ft. 3 in. long from the pin to its after edge by 3 ft. 3 in. wide. The skeg also has plenty of area as well as the rudder. This particular design shows rather more flare in the topsides than usually carried by the small working boats of the Chesapeake; therefore the bottom has less width in relation to the water line length and consequently the boat has less displacement and will carry a smaller load than the original from which it has been developed. However since this is a yacht the paying load matters little, and the performance under sail will be better for the change. There should be close to 1,200 pounds of inside ballast, this to be small pigs of lead and stowed both sides of the centerboard trunk. with perhaps a few hundred pounds between the mast step and the trunk to counterbalance the weight of several people in the cockpit.

The rig is a replica of those carried by these smart little boats, and a most practical rig it is too. The sharp rake of the mast gives a rakishness sadly lacking in the conventional single stickers that have become the mode today. While the mast is stepped well forward, thanks to the rake, the center of the mainsail lies well aft. Also because of the steep rake the leach of the mainsail stands more nearly vertical than it otherwise would. The advantage of this is that the leech will not roll over; therefore sail battens are not required. The area of the mainsail is 265 sq. ft. The luff of the mainsail is held to the mast with wooden hoops; those below the third row of reef points being secured by a jack rope; and those above lashed to grommets in the sail. The jib is hanked to the headstay which, by the way, leads from the mast, thence through a sheave in the bow sprit, and is then made fast to the cutwater with a suitable turnbuckle. Thus when lowered the jib will fall all the way to the bowsprit and not land on top of some offending turnbuckle or other superfluous fitting. The foot of the jib carries a club. In addition to the headstay there is a topmast stay which leads to the tip of the bowsprit and made fast with a turnbuckle.

DETAILS OF THE CENTERBOARD; A DRAWING SHOWING THE CONSTRUCTOIN AT THE RAISED DECK; SECTION AT STATION 6 SHOWING THE CENTERBOARD TRUNK, THE SIDE DECKS, AND THE ARRANGEMENT OF THE CABIN DOORS.

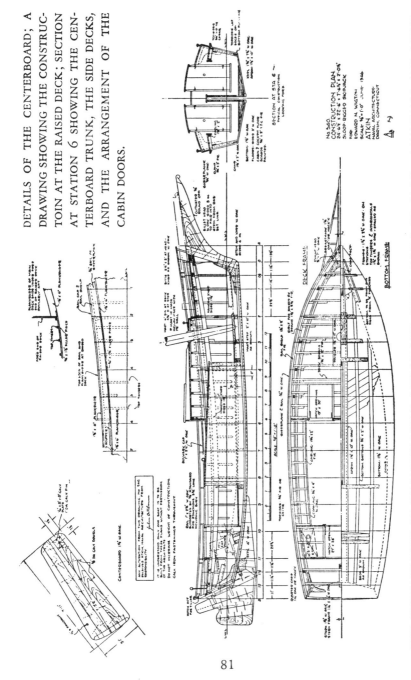

THE SKIPJACK WILL BE STRONGLY BUILT, DESPITE THE ELIMINATION OF COSTLY MATERIALS AND METHODS OF CONSTRUCTION.

Thence from the bowsprit eye band a chain bob-stay leads to the cut-water. Shipshape and practical this is and exactly in keeping with the spirit of the whole design. The jib has an area of 108 sq. ft. which gives the skipjack a total area of 370 sq. ft. of sail. It is interesting to point out that both the mainsail and jib carry lazy jacks, and it is well worth studying the lead of those on the jib. I sometimes wonder when it blows how the present generation of helmsmen manage to tuck in reefs when it really freshens up, because few of the frail craft they sail carry lazyjacks. The sails for a boat like this new one for Mr. Wigton should have cloths running with the leeches, should be properly roped, be laced to the boom and club, and have reefing tackle rove, at least for the first row of reef points, in the mainsail. Six ounce domestic duck is about the right material for the sails.

The mast will be solid and should be made from a natural stick of spruce. It will be 6 in. in dia. at the deck, tapering to 3 in. dia. at the band for the main halyard block. Two shrouds are shown each side, both leading to the mast cleats that carry the eye splice in the jib stay: 5/16 in. dia. galvanized iron wire is specified for shrouds and jib stay, the topmost stay being made of $\frac{1}{4}$ in. dia. wire. Shrouds will have deadeyes and lanyards leading to the chain plates. Landlubberly persons will scoff at these; but never-the-less how well they harmonize with the friendly little hooker.

The running rigging will all be nice comfortable-to-the-hands Manila rope; if you can show me anything better for a little ship I should like to see it. I have experimented with this stuff called — rope; it is a very poor substitute for Manila or hemp cordage. I have found it is bitching stuff to splice, it stretches out of all conscience, it frays out, it is slippery to the hands and to cleats and winches, the white variety soon becomes as dirty as a tramp's shirt and the khaki dyed variety fits the army camp better than the spars of a yacht. It is stronger for equal size to other cordage but since there must always be a generous margin of safety this is a matter of little import as it concerns the rigging of a cruising yacht. And besides, running rigging of large diameter is much easier to haul and hold with the hands than small stuff; this is one of the reasons why the main sheets are usually rove with a man's size piece of Manila or hemp rope.

The deck of the sucessor to *Tally Ho!* will be raised from station 2 to station 6, its beams span the tops of the bulwark rail each side; with the crown shown head room is provided for the cuddy. Not

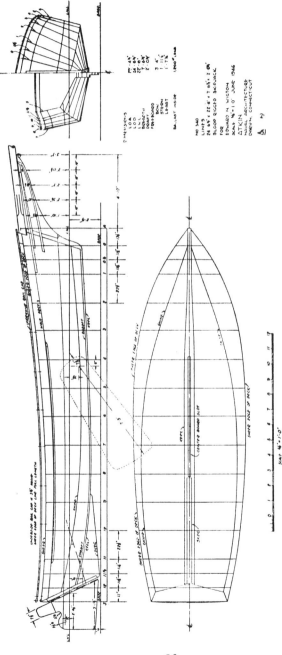

THE LINES OF THE 22 FT. 6 IN. WATER LINE SKIPJACK DESIGNED BY ATKIN & CO., FOR MR. E. N. WIGTON, HUNTINGTON, L. I., N. Y. THE PRINCIPAL DIMENSIONS OF THE BOAT ARE: LENGTH ON DECK, 24 FT. 6½ IN.; LENGTH ON WATER LINE, 22 FT. 6 IN.; BREADTH ON DECK, 7 FT. 6½ IN.; AND DRAFT, 2 FT. ½ IN.

the headroom for standing up because the cuddy is intended only as a place to tuck into in case of rain and a place in which to change from shore to working clothes. A sliding hatchway is shown each side the center board trunk and beneath these about 4 ft. of headroom, so you see the little shelter will not be too uncomfortable. There will be a well deck forward and this gives protection to the gear required for anchoring and mooring. The bulwark rail and pipe rail above it, stand nearly a foot above the deck and this will give an idea of the shelter one has when the time comes to break out an anchor when the weather is bad.

The cockpit will be 7 ft. 4 in. long and 5 ft. wide inside the low coamings. The side decks here drop to the level of the sheer line and continue thus to the stern. There is a seat shown each side the cockpit and both these are placed well down in the boat, giving comfort and security to helmsman and crew. The centerboard trunk will of course extend into the cockpit, but this cannot be avoided in a boat of this kind. The space beneath the after deck will house the engine. The sharp shaft angle may be criticized but I can assure the skeptics that I have made installations exactly like this in many other small auxiliarys with excellent results. Providing the engine has a lubricating system that will pump oil to the bearings the arrangement shown will be satisfactory despite the angle at which it is installed. The engine shown on the plans is a 2 h.p. single cylinder four cycle model and in the past has functioned perfectly installed as indicated. With the slide in the after deck and doors opening into the cockpit the engine is always easy to get at for starting or adjustments. The gasoline tank will be located under the deck and will have a capacity of approximately 6 gals. Personally I should be disposed to have the engine direct connected to the shaft without a clutch or reverse gear; much simpler this way and once one becomes accustomed to such an arrangement handling the little boat under power will be child's play.

The construction of the skipjack will not follow the practice of the Chesapeake Bay builders, and this especially in the matter of the keel and deadwood. The plans as drawn show a keel made of 1¾ thick by 7½ in. wide white oak. This will be bent to the sweep of the bottom and will be over-laid with an apron piece made of 1½ in. by 10 in. wide white oak, the two pieces to be screw fastened after each has been bent to the proper sweep of the bottom. The slot for the centerboard will be sawn and the trunk made and fitted, but not as yet fastened to the keel. This should be done after the bottom planking is on and the side frames have been set up. The chine pieces will be made of 1⅛ in. by 3 in. white oak and will be let into the heels of the side frames as shown at station 6. The bottom planking will be laid diagonally from the keel to the chine pieces and will be made of 1⅛ in. thick white oak in widths of about 5 in. There will be two bottom battens each side made of ¾ in. by 3 in. white oak, screw fastened to the bottom planking. The floor timbers will be made of 3 in. white oak and set as shown and made to the depths indicated on the plans. The side frames will be made of 1¼ in. by 2½ in. white oak and will be placed on 11¼ in. centers. The clamps will be made of 1⅛ in by 4 in. fir and will be screw fastened to the frames. The topside planking will be made of ¾ in. thick white cedar or clear fir and should be in strakes not more than 4½ in. wide at their widest point. Fasten side planking with screws; the seams are to be caulked and properly payed and stopped with Ferdico flexible seam composition. The deck beams will be made of 1½ in. by 2 in. fir set on the centers shown and both the main and raised decks will be laid with ¾ in. by 2 in. white pine or edge grain fir; the seams to be caulked, payed and stopped with Ferdico seam putty. Sheer planks, hatches, rail caps, and all outside joiner work will be made of clear white oak. The above, then is briefly the way the construction of this interesting little auxiliary yacht will be handled.

And so we have the highlights and the plans of a very genuine kind of cruising boat which someday will be built to cruise in waterways unknown to long legged yachts like *Tally Ho!*.

A fair day single-handed

Bull Frog

Designed by **William Garden**

THE writer has long been an admirer of William Garden's designs. They all have a great amount of character and a practical look seldom found these days. When the BOOK OF BOATS was conceived Mr. Garden's name was one of the foremost in our minds to ask for contributions in the way of designs. Therefore, it is logical for *Bull Frog* to appear in The FIRST BOOK OF BOATS and in the future we are looking forward to seeing more of this Pacific coast designer's work.

He recently sent us the accompanying design with a brief description—"I have enclosed a little cat schooner which, while not practical for the average cruising man, should nevertheless prove quite interesting since sailing workboats are becoming a rarity. The trollers of the west coast range from 26 ft. to 50 ft. and some of them are the finest small seagoing power boats imaginable. A riding fore sail is carried ordinarily, but occasionally a jib-and-mainsail boat may be seen.

Recently on the west coast there has been a trend of interest toward sail and several sailing fishermen are planned. The schooner rig seems best adaptable since the mast locations work in well with the fisherman's deck arrangements and the foresail is quite handy when under power. *Bull Frog's* scantlings are fairly representative for her size."

In connection with "sailing fishermen" and sailing workboats in general, it is interesting that the designer writes, "there has been a trend of interest toward sail and several sailing fishermen are planned." Such boats as the Friendship sloops, the New Haven sharpies, the Chesapeake Bay bugeyes, the Gloucester fishermen and others too innumerable to list, earned "their keep" and a substantial living for their respective crews and owners for many years. These, for the main part, have slowly disappeared and gasoline and diesel powered fishermen are off the banks, shoals and inlets taking the fish. It may be barely possible that this "modern" fishing fleet is not as efficient as it is assumed to be and that the old-time sailer may return once again. For, after all, trolling under sail day in and day out would be very inexpensive in comparison to turning over a 150 h.p. gasoline or diesel engine by any manner of figuring. It must be brought to mind, however, that considerable time is saved with power fishing vessels in going to and returning from the fishing

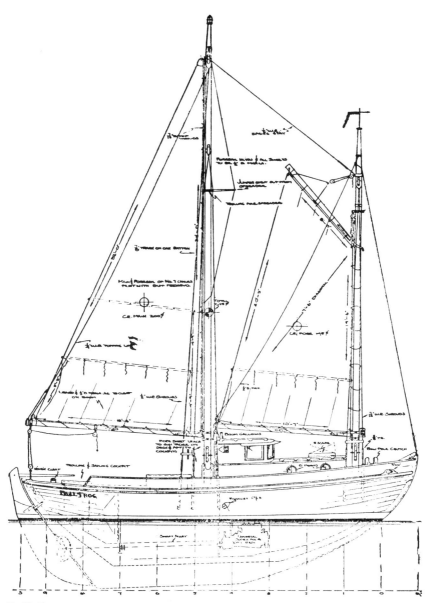

Bull Frog IS THE WORK OF MR. WILLIAM GARDEN OF SEATTLE, WASH-
INGTON. SHE IS A CAT-SCHOONER AND IS UNIQUE IN BEING A PRESENT
DAY EXAMPLE OF A SAILING-WORKBOAT.

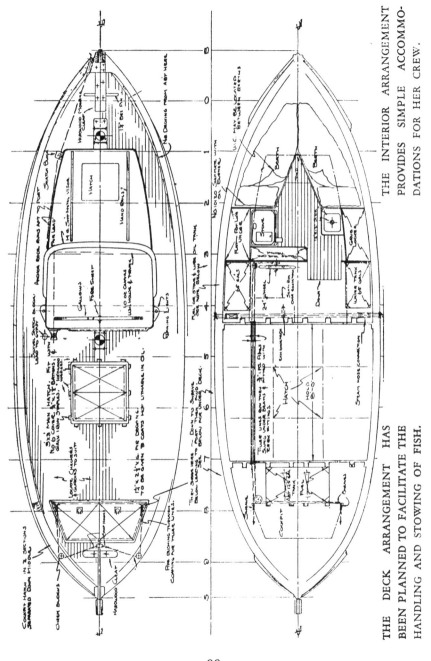

THE INTERIOR ARRANGEMENT PROVIDES SIMPLE ACCOMMODATIONS FOR HER CREW.

THE DECK ARRANGEMENT HAS BEEN PLANNED TO FACILITATE THE HANDLING AND STOWING OF FISH.

88

grounds. This thought is introduced only as a matter of interest—and possibly to open the matter to further discussion and consideration.

The frames are 1⅞ in. sq. white oak on 12 in. centers. Planking is shown 1¼ in. thick and the ceiling is ¾ in. thick with a bilge stringer made up of four lengths of 1¼ in. by 3 in. fir. The rest of the scantlings are correspondingly heavy and it is evident that these little boats are built to take the severe weather often experienced on the west coast.

An interesting feature is a cast concrete keel. Unfortunately Mr. Garden didn't tell us its weight but it is loaded with boiler punchings and through-bolted to a 7½ in. keel.

The interior arrangement is simple. Accommodations for two men, including two berths, a galley and lockers, are forward. Abaft this, under the pilot house deck, with a third, aft. These three tanks have duction gear provides power. At 1600 r.p.m. 6 knots cruising speed is available. The exhaust leads out each side, and therefore, since both outlets cannot be submerged when the little ship rolls, there cannot be back pressure in the exhaust line.

There are two fuel tanks to port and starboard, which are also under the pilot house deck, with a third, aft. These three tanks have a capacity of 255 gals. of gasoline, sufficient for a wide cruising radius. The "pay space" consists of a cargo hold 8 ft. long and the full breadth of the boat.

A small cockpit in the aft deck is used while sailing and trolling.

Twin trolling poles are secured for sea at the spreader on the mainmast. They are each 32 ft. long. Two additional trolling poles are located on the foremast. When trolling, these poles are rested in the crutches provided at the rail, outboard of their respective masts.

Bull Frog has a sail area of 345 sq. ft. in her two working sails; 200 sq. ft. in the mainsail, and 145 sq. ft. in the fore. While *Bull Frog* is strictly a sailing work boat, it is very easy to see the possibilities of her being a particularly attractive and practical auxiliary sailing yacht.

The sail plan, unlike the commonplace, has many advantages for a cruising boat. Among other things, it is all inboard, it is easily shortened in case of hard winds, it provides excellent balance because the little ship will handle well with either main or fore, or with both. Off the wind with fore and main sails "wong" out all the sail area becomes effective; and if the wind freshens, one does not have to worry about getting in a delicate spinnaker or balloon jib, as might be the case with a more orthodox rig. *Bull Frog* will jog along beautifully under

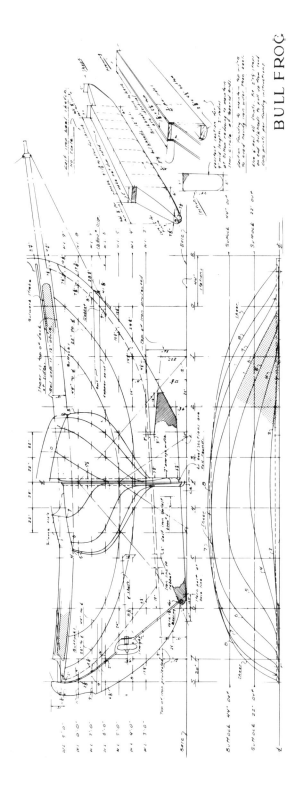

BULL FROG

THE LINES OF A LATER VERSION OF THE *Bull Frog*. THIS ONE HAS SHARPER FORWARD WATERLINES, FLATTER QUARTERS, SLIGHTLY MORE BREADTH ON THE WATERLINE, AND, FOR THIS BURDENSOME A HULL, AN EASY RUN.

foresail alone and this handy sail is perfect for steadying purposes while the boat is proceeding under power.

This "sailing workboat" has an overall length of 32 ft. 0 in.; is 27 ft. on the load water line; her breadth is 10 ft. 6 in.; and she draws 5 ft. 0 in. of water loaded to her designed water line.

When I first saw the designs of *Bull Frog* I was impressed with her ship-shape and very practical appearance. She looks like a grand little boat and one that would be fun to own.

Mr. Cleat

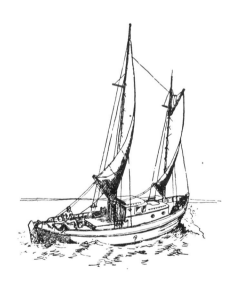

Small boats arc welded

William Atkin

WITH all too few exceptions, small yachts and boats have always been built from wood and most yachtsmen, being conservative, are not easily influenced by the many excellent aspects of metallic hulls.

However, during the last two years an increasing number of inquiries have come to my office in connection with a proper design for a small boat to be built from metal, welded metal, galvanized iron, steel, bronze, and aluminum.

Most of my clients are amateur boat builders. In recent years with the production of inexpensive arc welding outfits, the urge has come to build from wooden boat construction plans using metal in large pieces in place of the thousands of pieces of wood and fastenings that enter into the building of wooden craft.

One of these amateur builders, Mr. W. I. Nichol, Saugus, Mass., has built two small boats adapted from wooden construction. One an 18-foot V-bottom auxiliary designed by the late C. D. Mower, the other a 23-ft. double-end V-bottom runabout from my design. For both these Mr. Nichol has great praise. Of the latter, he writes that in the hurricane of September, 1938, his galvanized Armco iron arc welded runabout, *Needle,* was washed ashore before the great wind and tremendous sea, grounding among a forest of jagged boulders and small rocks making up the beach. Excepting for dents and scratched-off paint the boat was undamaged structurally. Its motor and equipment were ruined with salt water corrosion. Shaft, propeller, strut and rudder were badly bent. Within a week, the iron-hulled *Needle* was about its tasks again, little worse for her violent experience. Every other of the dozens of small wooden boats that were washed ashore in the locality were smashed into kindling wood, and total losses.

It is interesting to note that Mr. Nichol's runabout was built from galvanized iron, the decks approximately 1/16 in. thick; sides and bottom plating approximately 1/10 in. thick. There are no frames, floor timbers, stem, stern, or keel in the construction. Deck beams are the only framing used and these are very light.

When completed and with same motor and equipment specified for the wooden hull, the little boat rested exactly on her designed water

THE SAIL PLAN OF THE LITTLE ARC
WELDED STEEL SLOOP CARRIES
194 SQ. FT.; 51 SQ. FT. IN THE
JIB, 143 SQ. FT. IN THE MAIN
SAIL. THE MASTING AND
STANDING RIGGING HAS A
NOTE OF COMPLETE SIMPLI-
CITY; JUST TWO SHROUDS
AND A SINGLE HEAD STAY.
WHILE THE SAIL AREA
IS MODEST IT IS AMPLE
FOR CRUISING.

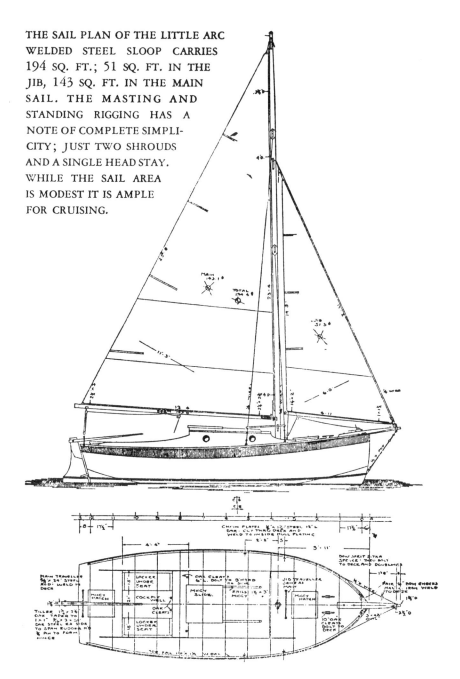

line indicating the construction in steel came to exactly the same weight as construction in wood. The boat also made the speed specified for the wooden hull, which is of considerable interest.

A metal hull will not leak if arc welded, and cannot sink if fitted with flotation tanks or water tight compartments. These seem priceless advantages for the metal welded hull.

How long will a steel hull last plated with sheets less than 1/8 in. thickness? Given reasonable care, just as long as a wooden hull of similar characteristics. I am reminded of this fact often having advised one of my clients not to spend good money on the conversion of a World War I galvanized iron life boat. That will have been 20, or more, years ago. The old life boat is still going. I am afraid I was taking too seriously the advice of conservative contemporaries.

A year or so ago another client, Mr. Wayne Backus, Winniwicee, Washington, asked me to design him a 16 ft. V-bottom runabout, the boat to be built in a small welding shop by an amateur builder. This boat was not an adaptation from a conventional wooden design.

The hull was built from six sheets of Armco galvanized iron, the bottom and side plating being 12 ga. and the deck and bulkheads 14 ga. Deck beams, tabs, etc. were made from cuttings from the side and deck plates. Four sheets for the sides and bottom were 24 in. and 36 in. wide respectively, while two sheets for the deck were 36 in. wide. All sheets were 17 ft. long. The little boat turned out very well, performed exactly like the more usual wooden types. Like the two hulls built by Mr. Nichol, the 16 ft. runabout was built without frames, keel, deadwood, clamps, knees, shelves, floor timbers, etc., parts which are always associated with the construction of wooden hulls.

Early in 1940 I completed a third design for Mr. Nichol, this one a V-bottom auxiliary gaff-headed sloop 18 ft. 9 in. over all, 17 ft. 6 in. water line, 6 ft. beam, and 3 ft. draft. The breadth was kept to 6 ft. because sheet iron of this width and 20 ft. long was available.

The design of the 17 ft. 6 in. water line steel cruising sloop, (see Figs. 1, 2, 3 and 4) was made several months ago.

* * * * *

Having been in the profession of naval architecture for many years, it seems certain to me that the only way in which "everyman's" boat can be produced is to build it of steel. It is impossible to build wooden hulls inexpensively. There are too many parts to be shaped and handled, and

94

wood is too flexible to handle cheaply in forming the hull of so complicated a form as a boat.

In the past the trouble with building small steel hulls has been that they were put together in the same manner as wooden hulls, and not in the manner of a tank or box. Therefore, with all the customary parts used in old-fashioned boat building nothing was saved in time and the completed hull was entirely too heavy. It is astonishing to me that so many moderate sized welded steel hulls are built today with so many unnecessary parts—positively steeped in tradition both as to form and construction.

My tabloid sailing boat has dimensions as follows: length over all, 19 ft. 8 in.; length water line, 17 ft. 6 in.; breadth, 7 ft.; draft 2 ft. 11 in. The freeboard at the bow is 3 ft. 2½ in.; at the lowest point, 2 ft. 2 in.; at the stern, 2 ft. 4¼ in. The displacement is 4,100 lbs.; sail area, 194.4 sq. ft.; and ballast, all inside, 1,200 lbs. And by the way, this is my 490th design since going into business 34 years ago.

* * * * *

It is difficult for the layman to realize that a hull plated with 12 ga. rolled iron or steel will weigh about the same as a hull planked with three layers diagonally of a total thickness of 1⅛ in. of white oak. And this would be considered exceedingly heavy for a small boat like the subject of this paper. If built of weldwood this thickness floor timbers, stringers etc., would be unnecessary deadwood. But one cannot build a boat with weldwood without stringers, keel, chine pieces, deadwood, and all the parts that make up the hull of a wooden boat. Only the fitting and forming of frames is saved in plywood hulls, and the plywood must be screwed or glued to something to maintain its position and shape. And then, of course, there are thousands of wood screws or copper rivets to be bored for and driven before your wooden hull is completed, a time-consuming job.

Items to be made, handled and fitted in wooden hull of this type and size are: 30 planks, 28 battens, 42 deck planks, 2 pieces canvas with glue and tacks, 1 keel, 3 pieces deadwood with 26 bolts, 3 pieces in stem, 11 pieces in stern, 2 clamps, 2 shelves, each made from two lengths, 3 knees, 24 chine knees, 2 rabbeted chine logs, 48 bolts in keel, stem, stern assembly, 12 floor timbers, 16 butt blocks, 7 doublings, 5 pieces in rudder. 18 deck beams and headers. 6 pieces half round sheer moulding, plus 3,230 fastenings of five different sizes with wooden plugs to

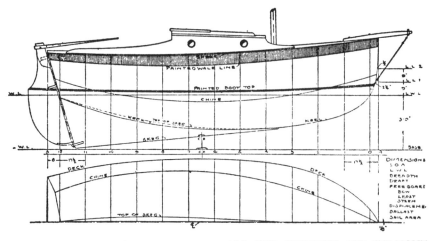

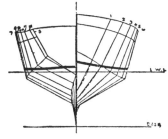

ALL THE SECTIONS ARE STRAIGHT LINES. HOWEVER THE THREE FORWARD SECTIONS BELOW THE CHINES WILL SHOW CONVEXITY AFTER THE PLATING IS LAID. THERE IS NO HARM IN THIS AND SINCE THERE ARE NO FRAMES IN THE HULL THE PLATING CAN BE LEFT TO TAKE ITS NATURAL FORM. THIS HAS PROVED TO BE GOOD PRACTICE.

cover countersinks over heads, making a grand total hull lumber and fastenings, 3,495 pieces not including boat plugs which will come to at least 1,200 more.

Items to be cut, handled and fitted in arc welded iron or steel hull of similar size and type to above are: 2 pieces 36 in. by 20 ft. 12 ga. plate for sides; 2 pieces 40 in. wide by 20 ft. long 12 ga. plate for bottom; 2 pieces 36 in. wide by 12 ft. long 12 ga. plate for skeg; 2 pieces 40 in wide by 20 ft. long 14 ga. plate for deck; 1 piece 52 in. wide by 10 ft. long 12 ga. plate for cockpit bottom and sides; 1 piece 20 in. wide by 6 ft. long 12 ga. plate for rudder; 1 piece 36 in. wide by 5 ft. long 12 ga. plate for stern; 34 deck beams and headers made from scrap from side plating, 12 ga. plate 1 1/2 in. and 1 in. respectively; 4 butt plates under center seam in deck; making a total of 48 pieces required.

The above tabulation concerns only the hull with rudder. However the interior fittings and rig in either wood or metal hulls will require about the same materials and time to complete.

If only one hull is considered, it should be built over wooden forms made in the same manner as for wooden boats. Use spruce about 1 1/8 in. thick for the forms and brace well both to floor and to each other. If duplication is required in quantities it would be best to build the forms from steel plates and shapes. A form must be made for each of the stations shown on the drawing of the lines. And the lines should always be drawn (or laid down) full size. Too much care cannot be given this part of the work.

Since there is no keel in this type construction the forms should be set up upside down, that is with the deck down. The simplest way to do this is to set up blocking for each station so that the tops of these form the sheer line in an upside down position. Set the blocks at convenient height to work comfortably. Raise the forms sufficiently high from the floor to allow for a strong batten 6 or 8 in. above the line of the sheer. This will give better working room in fitting the plates. Also run battens, let in flush, two each side for both bottoms and sides. These will brace the forms. Fasten with wood screws.

It is good practice to saw a piece of 1/2 in. plywood to the curve of the keel and stem from station 2 forward as a guide or pattern for cutting and fitting the forward ends of the side and bottom plates. This should be placed about 1 1/2 in. abaft the cutwater of the stem; it will be inside the hull when the plating is on.

V-bottom models with straight sections are ideal for building with welded metal. One bend only is required of the plating and none will have to be furnace heated and rolled and hammered into place. You will notice there are dotted lines indicating slight convex below the chine at stations 1, 2 and 3. The steel will take this form naturally and the sections will appear to be perfectly straight. This is the way it is intended.

V-bottom models are also excellent performers in rough water and equally as fast as round bilge craft, provided, of course, that the design is of correct form for both types.

The topsides of the sailing boat will be made from 12 ga. iron or steel plate. It can be had in a single piece. If butted plates are needed see detail for this joint on the construction-cabin plan. For the amateur builder, it may be well to mention that plating of this thickness must be cut with powers shears or with the welding outfit. Shears will be best, I feel, for this particular work.

97

The surest and best way to obtain the exact shape of each plate is to make patterns from hard strong cardboard. Since both sides of the hull must be alike, patterns should be made for one side only. Lay pattern on the plate with colored pencil or scriber. Mark the position of each form. Bore holes for wood screws along the sheer edge of the plate and at the edge of the chine at each mould. Also bore holes about 5 in. apart along the stem approximately 1 in. abaft the cutwater, also at the top and bottom of the stern end of the plate. One-quarter in. bolts and screws will be inserted in these to hold the side plates in correct position until welded together. Clamps can be used here to advantage also. All the plates will have square edges, tops, bottoms, and ends, no bevels required. In welding, the welding rod will build up a neat rounded bead, entirely filling the seam or joint between the plate edges.

Both halves of the bottom plating will be treated in the same manner and will be made for the same thickness iron or steel plate.

The stern will be made from 12 ga. plate and will be temporarily fastened with screws, bolted and clamped in exact position, then arc welded to the sides and bottom. Leave all edges square in same manner as on sides and bottom plating.

If welding is neatly and properly done it will be best to leave joinings in natural state without grinding or filing smooth. The scale left by the heat will rust much less than bright surface.

Cementing and painting will form a very smooth and fair surface and the beaded corners of chines, cutwater, and at the stern will look business-like and neat. It may be well to mention that an iron hull should not be painted with the usual copper anti-fouling compositions used so successfully on wooden hulls, so do not use any paint that contains copper, aluminum or brass. The finest quality red lead in oil is best for priming coat, and apply two thin coats rather than one thick coat slapped on in a hurry, followed by at least four coats of gloss outside yacht paint. Anti-fouling white composition will be best for underwater portions.

Deck beams will be made from 12 ga. plate. Those of the main deck will be 1½ in. deep and will be spaced on every station with one between. The crown of the beams will be 2 in. in a length of 4 ft. The ends of the beams will be arc welded to the inner face of the side plating at the sheer. Hatch headers, cabin house carlins, cockpit floor beams will be of the same dimensions.

Cockpit floor and sides with cabin sides and ends will be made

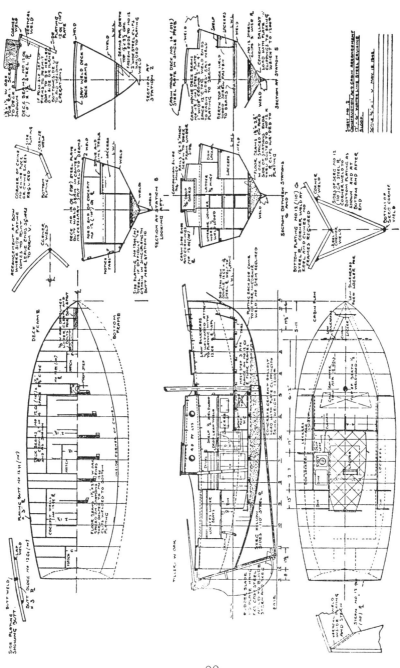

99

THERE IS LITTLE NEED OF FRAMES, CLAMPS, STRINGERS, DEADWOOD, OR KEEL IN A SMALL ARC WELDED HULL.

from 12 ga. plate, also cockpit coamings. Floor of cockpit is flat and the beams should extend full across the hull having ends welded to side plating.

The deck will be made from 14 ga. plate. It will be difficult to get plate in this thickness 7 ft. wide and so it will be necessary to run a seam through the middle line of the deck. Use corner weld for fastening deck to side plating and spot-weld from under side to deck beams. Cabin house top will be made the same but the beams here will be 1 in. in depth and set on 12 in. centers.

The sides of the open skeg will be made from 12 ga. plate and formed and fitted to hull as clearly indicated on the plans.

Rudder will be 12 ga. plate. It would be well to fit cheek pieces made from white oak each side the rudder to give it thickness to support the tiller which will be 1 3/4 in. thick. Then the side plates on tiller that form the hinge will exactly span the rudder head and form a very solid fitting.

It being impractical to finish the interior in iron or steel plate it will be necessary to weld tabs made from 14 ga. plate to give attachment places for the various wooden members of the joiner work. Through-bolt wood to the tabs wherever possible. Then everything can be removed if it is ever necessary to repaint the interior or chip off scale. But this operation will be a long, long way down the wind if the boat is half way cared for. One half-inch thick weldwood is excellent material for constructing the interior joiner work.

And there we have the hull for a very nice little cruising boat.

Ballast will be cement loaded with scrap pieces of plating.

The cabin is designed for two, and has everything needed for comfortable living and sailing. Provision is made for installation of pump water closet if this is needed. One cannot expect full headroom in a small boat like this and so long as there is full sitting up headroom the cabin will be found to be snug and homelike. And whatever the weather outside, you can be sure the deck house, decks and arc welded steel hull will be absolutely watertight at all times. This is a comfort in any type cruising boat.

The rig is the accepted type today with tall mast, and short foot, altogether proved and accepted as efficient as the rig for a small sailing boat can be.

The time required for building the hull with decks, deck house, cockpit, hatches, companion slides, ballast, toe rails, and rudder of a standard type wooden hull of 4,100 lbs. displacement will be very close to four weeks with two experienced boat builders, or approximately 384 hours, provided the materials are first class and proper tools available. At 80 cents an hour this is $307.00

First class boat building lumber for the hull as above will cost at retail, $210.00, fastenings, caulking cotton, boat plugs very close to $40.00. Thus, the hull complete, $250, with labor, $547.

The hull completed represents very close to 2/5ths the cost of the whole outfit, joiner work, fittings, spars, rigging, sails, and painting will bring the complete boat to a figure of $1,365. And this will be a good average price in normal times for a boat builder with a good reputation for good work and materials.

The time required for building an arc welded steel hull of the same displacement and model will be very close to ten days with two experienced steel boat builders and welders, or approximately 160 hours, providing the steel plates were of specified sizes and proper tools were on hand to produce the work. At 80 cents an hour this is $120.

The steel plates for the hull completed to the same point as the wooden hull will cost $136 including welding rod. Electric current will add close to $20 at local rates. Thus, the arc welded hull complete with labor, would cost $276.

The boat then completed with arc welded steel hull and equipment exactly the same as the wooden boat above will have a cost of $1,084, a saving of $271; or slightly less than 20 per cent.

In the plans, the conventional symbols for welding have been omitted as being of little use to the amateur welder, and the professional welder will consider the job a simple straight-forward bit of work that can be done blindfolded.

From the above one can see the possibilities of great savings in labor and materials if small simple boats are built from iron or steel arc welded.

The above article appeared in STUDIES IN ARC WELDING published in 1943 by The James F. Lincoln Arc Welding Foundation, Cleveland, Ohio, and received for its author the FIRST PRIZE on the subject of PLEASURE WATERCRAFT.

A letter

Dear Mr. Atkin,

A COPY of January '45 MOTOR BOATING has finally made its way around the world, (the hard way—I could have made the same time with a dory) and I am writing to congratulate you on your design for that month's issue—the utility boat *Tanja*.

Your remarks with reference to building practice—necessity for floors and knees and adequate mast steps—are most pertinent. I know too well the shoddy method you decry.

One of my favorite dreams with a strong element of the practical, actually, is owning and living upon a very lovely Island East of Penobscot Bay, Maine. I have annexed *Tanja* for this dream. She would be the ideal utility boat for the Maine coast for an island home. Fall and winter see weather there that is utterly beyond the comprehension of the average "summer" people.

The 5 h.p. heavy duty engine suggested is ideal. I installed a 52 h.p. high speed engine in a 33 ft. Jonesport Lobster boat and was startled to have the same model boat prove faster with a slow turning 40 h.p. marine engine.

I realize that you get a great deal of gratuitous advice, and requests for some, along the line "I like such and such a sailing skiff but why not enlarge her 60% all around; then I can install my model 1922 Pierce Arrow Engine! What size propeller should I use? etc. etc." I cannot resist a wistful statement, however, that a motor-boat approximately as per attached sketch, with lines fulfilling the characteristics of *Tanja,* and with construction on a similar scale, would make the ideal all weather Maine Coast fishing, camping, and "party" boat. The 40 h.p. motor mentioned above with 18 in. wheel at 1400 might net 10 knots. 10 knots is damn fast—I have always found that 8 knots is usually estimated (by owner) as "about fifteen".

I wish to assure you again of the high "morale factor" contained in your boat designs in addition to their superior architectural merit.

Sincerely,

William Law
Lt. Col. FA
Bangkok, Siam

102

"The ideal all weather Maine Coast boat –"

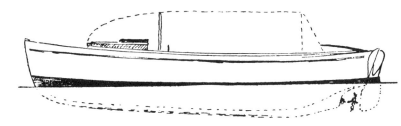

"I have annexd *Tanja*
for this dream"
30 ft. 6 in. o.a. by 28 ft.
6 in. with 8 ft. 6 in. beam and 2 ft. 8 in. draft.

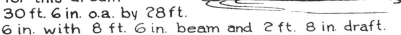

"battened canvas cover will give protection."

Petrel--a boat of yesterday

Designed by John Hyslop

THE yacht *Petrel* was designed in 1876 by the late Mr. John Hyslop of New York, and built under his supervision that same winter by Mr. Wm. T. Johnson at Port Richmond, Staten Island, New York. The designer spent many years experimenting with various hull forms in obtaining, to his satisfaction, some of the answers to the "wave-line area" theory. In *Petrel* the cross areas, as shown, were regulated by this method and correspond to the ordinates of a "wave-curve". Not only are the cross areas regulated by this method, but all the waterlines are in themselves wave-lines.

Whether *Petrel* owed her success to this theory, or merely to the fact that she was clean cut in form and beautifully proportioned is hardly open to question. A very different boat may have resulted from a person of less experience than Mr. Hyslop. Even had that person lived up in full to the theory of wave-line design. After all the original choice of displacement, the principal dimensions and general features of the yacht are matters of judgment for which no governing formulae are in existence.

A study of her lines, on page 117, will show that for a boat of her depth *Petrel* had particularly sweet fore and aft sections and diagonals. Her flare forward was ample to lift her dry and clear in rough water, drawn in just enough to clear the water flowing under her stern. *Petrel's* moderate beam and "even ends" insured a generally fine form. The principal dimensions were 32 ft. over all; 28 ft. on the waterline. Her extreme beam was 8 ft. on the waterline. And her draft was 4 ft. 7 in. at the deepest point. She displaced 7½ tons with 5,474 lbs. of lead on her keel and 2,526 lbs. of inside ballast, properly distributed.

Petrel was a cutter in point of principle, though she had some of the mechanical features of a sloop of her period. Her working sails had a total area of 800 sq. ft. distributed in the mainsail, with 522 sq. ft., the foresail with 132 sq. ft., and the jib with 146 sq. ft. They were perfectly proportioned and, as the sail plan shows, she was a particularly attractive boat. According to her history, in actual sailing she was

Petrel's SAIL PLAN IS A COMPROMISE BETWEEN THAT OF AN AMERICAN SLOOP AND THAT OF AN ENGLISH CUTTER. HER MAST IS STEPPED SOMEWHAT FARTHER FORWARD THAN WAS CONSIDERED GOOD PRACTICE FOR A CUTTER BUT THE RIG ITSELF HAS ALL THE EARMARKS OF THE EXCELLENT SEA-GOING RIG OF THE LATTER; FIDDED TOPMAST, LARGE FORE TRIANGLE WITH DOUBLE HEADSAILS, MAINSAIL OF GENEROUS AREA, AND A BIG SPRIT TOPSAIL. IT IS INTERESTING TO SEE A YACHT OF THIS SIZE FITTED WITH A PROPER BOWSPRIT AND LONG JIB BOOM.

105

one of the smartest and easiest boats imaginable in a seaway and though her lee decks were awash by the time she was fairly down to her bearings, she was surprisingly dry and very close winded when beating into a strong head sea. *Petrel* was an extremely able boat and even with a double reefed mainsail and full staysail she went to windward exceptionally fast and comfortably as well. The rig, because of the careful consideration in its design, looks shipshape, wholesome and, from a sea-going standpoint, very practical. With a light club on the foresail working in a bight on the sheet as a traveler the foresheet did not have to be touched in going to windward. The sail area was quite moderate for the boat's length and the spars light with beneficial effect in a head sea. And "when heeled down she went along about her business in holiday fashion without towing her helm over the weather quarter, and without any gymnastics to keep her on her course," as a critic of the times once wrote.

In her time *Petrel* was considered a very handsome and shipshape yacht. And she had all the desirable features yachtsmen of seventy years or so ago, expected. Her gaff-head mainsail, double headsails and sprit topsail may seem cumbersome and complicated today. But despite this, *Petrel* had individuality and character; features so much lacking in many of the super-efficient racing yachts of today. Be this as it may, *Petrel* admirably accomplished her designer's wishes and more than fulfilled her owner's requirements.

There has been little recorded in connection with the accommodations of *Petrel*. The cabin was arranged in a simple fashion, as near as we can gather. There were two berths, each 24 in. wide and 13 ft. long either side of the boat with 32 in. of open floor space in between these. The galley, located forward, was reached by a square hatch on the foredeck. It was fitted with all the necessary equipment, stowage space for utensils and other cookery things. Unfortunately very little information about her interior layout is known.

The delineator of the accompanying sail plan and lines was the late Mr. C. P. Kunhardt. Mr. Kunhardt was associated with FOREST & STREAM magazine regularly from 1878 to 1883. During this time he prepared hundreds of beautiful drawings and wrote many pages of interesting criticism for the column YACHTING AND BOATING which appeared frequently in the magazine.

One of his close associates of the time has written that Mr. Kunhardt made no claims as an artist but that he was, none-the-less, very

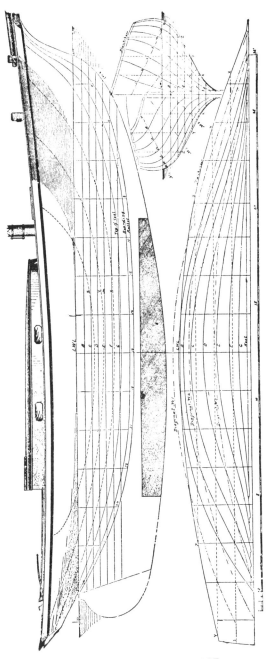

DRAWING OF THE LINES OF THE 28 FT. WATER LINE CUTTER, *Petrel*, DESIGNED IN 1876 BY THE LATE MR. JOHN HYSLOP. THE BUTTOCK LINES ARE OF PARTICULAR INTEREST; THESE HAVING SIMILAR CHARACTER-ISTICS BOTH FORWARD AND ABAFT THE MID SECTION, ALSO CONSIDERING THE YACHT'S DRAFT, THE BUT-TOCK LINES HAVE FAR MORE "FLATNESS" THAN FOUND IN MOST SAILING YACHTS OF TODAY. IN THE HALF BREADTH PLAN OF THE LINES ONE CAN DISTINCTLY SEE THE IDEA BEHIND THE "WAVE-FORM" OF THE WATER LINES; THERE IS BEAUTIFUL BALANCE BETWEEN THE ENDS OF THE HULL HERE. THE BODY PLAN SHOWS SECTIONS THAT HAVE PERFECT CONTINUITY FROM THE TOP OF THE CLIPPER STEM TO THE TIP OF THE NEATLY TURNED STERN TRANSOM. ALTOGETHER A FINE EXAMPLE OF YACHT DESIGNING.

skillful with the pen, and possessed of an artistic sense which was of great help in his work. All of his designs were supplemented by artistic shading and coloring which not only pleased the eye but made them better understood. His figure drawing was very crude, but when it came to the work which he loved best, the exaltation of the narrow cutter at her normal sailing angle of about 35 degrees, his portrayal was really artistic. Some might surpass his work in the actual lines drawn along a batten with a rightline pen, but he stood alone among naval architects in the line of artistic delineation. Mr. Kunhardt would report to work, at Forest & Stream, in the early evening, draw the night through, and leave a completed set of plans such as appear here, on his desk the following morning. An accomplishment not often done these days and, mind you, by the light of open gas jets, and the heat of an old fashioned office wood burning stove.

The lines and sailplans are reprinted from the pages of Mr. Kunhardt's SMALL YACHTS, THEIR DESIGN AND CONSTRUCTION, published in 1885 with the kind permission of the present proprietors.

Reeving off Jibtopsl Halliards

Part Two

Strong ripples

William Atkin

M Y old-time Shipmate, Alison McIver, and I used to ride around
visiting interesting Long Island boat shops, especially boat storage
yards, in a then new 1931 Chevrolet roadster. By the habits of
most good folk who love wholesome yachts and boats, Saturday after-
noons, Sundays and holidays would be the accepted time for this kind
of thing. Alison and I learned after a few years of this enchanting
pastime that a better time to visit boat yards was after dark at certain
phases of the moon and when a favoring winter wind sighed in from
the east.

From these excursions we began to suspect that boats in winter
storage *do not* sleep in silence. It is very evident the four winds of
heaven blow in and out the skirts which hang from winter covers and
rustle against the bilge poppets and tie-down lines. When the weather
is dry and the winds gentle, the sounds are soft; one, then, might think
spring hovered near. And when it is wet the tie-down lines and the
stiff canvas strum a harsh tune. Hard west winds shrill in the taut standing rigging and slat the running rigging left rove against the masts.
On very cold nights the icing on the tie-down lines and covers crackle
and scold. On those rare warm nights, which sometimes come in the
thaws of January, barely a whisper echos among the orderly rows of
boats snuggled together for a long winter's rest as though seeking protection against the winds, the cold, the rain, and the snow.

Continuing our search for further information in connection with
the subject in hand Alison and I turned the Chevrolet off the main highway leading from Huntington village to the Harbor and headed west
into the Mill Dam Road.

This turning off place *used* to be an enchanting place. Hard by the
bridge which spans Mill Creek was the house-boat home, yes, both winter and summer, of an old party known as Humpty-Dumpty and his
wife. There were several boats in various stages of delapidation made
fast to the east side of the creek; these, if you tarried there in the moon-
light or the half-light of evening, appeared rather shipshape, the whole
locality taking on a most eerie aspect then. We always felt this would
be a very unpromising time for inspecting or buying a second hand boat.

A few minutes drive to the westward brought us abreast the shop of Chute & Bixby, all dark and quiet inside with the moon-light dancing on the fast running water pouring from the nearby sluice gate of the mill pond. And in the door-yard of the shop stood two small cruising yachts in frame; one designed by Mr. John Alden, the other by me.

To the west of the shop between the mill pond and the harbor several winter-stored yachts snuggled together to protect themselves from the cold. It was the latter ones, my Shipmate and I had come to listen to, this winter night.

And what do boats—old ones and young ones—talk about? They will talk about themselves, their neighbors, their ailments, their hopes, their prospects, and their discouragements much the same as people talk. In passing it is refreshing to record that, excepting certain glittering needle-nosed ocean-racer cliques among them, there is nothing of boastfulness in the pixie-like nocturnal conversations among the winter time occupants of boat storage yards near and far. I am happy to add this is about what one would expect of honest, plain, wholesome, useful boats of which, fortunately, there are so very many.

A number of years ago my shipmate, Alison, settled down with a wife and family somewhere in the Chesapeake country and I forsook what once was known as Middle Riding for the charm of the state made famous by the manufacture of wooden nutmegs. In the passage of time the Chevrolet roadster has given over to a Jeep; a fresh air vehicle which is as open to the outdoors as the former and as much fun to drive.

So it came about on another memorable moonlit winter night, and in a new water-side terrain, the Jeep and I set out to listen to the gossip of some interesting little boats which I knew were standing in orderly rows in a boat yard, an hour's drive from Anchordown.

Among these was a very old 18-foot water line knockabout of 1900 vintage shivering uncovered in the cold moonlight; a dainty, if old, little open sailing boat well covered and well kept having all the earmarks of the hand of the Wizard of Bristol; one of Mr. Alden's *Malabar, Jrs.*, about twenty years old, a well preserved little auxiliary; a stout Nova Scotia built schooner about 26 ft. on deck used to the cold, but neverthe-less tucked in carefully against the weather; a John F. Small, circa 1910, gaff rigged cabin sloop; and some others, new and old, of various sizes and types; and most of these, for all their years, in sound condition. Among these boats stood a knockabout with the New Look and built of aluminum.

112

Despite the omens being favorable my visit to these wintering boats was disappointing. All were silent. To be sure the canvas covers swished in a kindly east wind, the tie lines slatted against the poppets, the rigging on the masts sang, but this night one could not, with certainty, fathom the meanings of the sounds.

Perhaps the youthfulness of the young aluminum lady, with the New Look, disturbed the sensibilities of the much older boats nearby. Old age may envy; but seldom is in harmony with youth or in sympathy with its gush, go and glitter. And since youth pays little heed to its elders anyway it may have been in retaliation that the Misses Crowinshield, Herreshoff, Small, Alden, Roue, Mower, and the other boats snuggling close in winter clothes kept counsel to themselves or spoke softly in mumble-jumble not wishing the very young to profit or understand.

I am not certain, but for a moment I thought I heard faint whispering in a high pitched voice intermingled with the noises of the winter covers and the words sounded like, "Do you think she of the New Look will last as long as you, Misses Mower, Small and Crowinshield?" Unfortunately I was unable to hear the replies of the three grand old maids because the whispers faded into the sigh of the wind and the sound of the wavelets washing along the shore.

Driving home, the Jeep and I tarried at an inviting place where the roadway skirts Long Island Sound, the sky was dazzling, the moon full and while we drank the sublimity of this old, but ever new, celestial panorama, five geese winging by in a single line were silhouetted against its face.

Continuing home I speculated as to whether the unusual sight of these five flying geese might not have significance? Might five be the answer to the whispered question put the Misses Mower, Small and Crowinshield?

We shall have to wait now for time to tell.

*   *   *

From whimsy, the Misses Crowinshield, et. al., moonlight, aluminum, and the New Look to Proceedings Second National Motor Boat Safety Conference is a long step indeed. The Safety Conference was held not long ago at New York and its purpose the discussion of measures which might be taken to make recreational boating an even safer outdoor pastime than it now is: and this will require a lot of "making".

In connection with fires and explosions on boats caused by badly tanked, piped and handled gasoline the expressions of Mr. H. A. Mur-

113

ray of The Texas Company at this meeting are especially interesting and worth careful consideration by all owners and operators of gasoline engined boats. Agreeing with Mr. Murray's practical views in the matter of gasoline, in boats, I am glad to record his words of wisdom here:

"Almost every one realizes that three conditions are necessary for a gasoline fire or explosion on a boat.

1. Presence of fuel.
2. Proper mixture of air and fuel.
3. A source of ignition.

"The explosive limits of air and gasoline vapor are roughly an air-fuel ratio (pounds of air per pound of fuel) of 5:1 on the rich side and 17:1 on the lean side. Mixtures of air and fuel which are richer or leaner than these cannot as a rule burn or explode.

"It is well to bear in mind these conditions inasmuch as they have a distinct bearing on the safety recommendations which might be drawn up by this panel, for example. Under normal conditions, the gasoline vapors in a partly filled fuel tank are too rich to burn or explode. Calculations and recent experimental laboratory tests show that, under sea level conditions and with either marine or aviation gasoline, the air-fuel mixture in the tank cannot burn or explode at temperatures down to approximately 10°F.

"This raises the question of whether it is necessary to extend the filler neck in the fuel tank all the way to the bottom of the tank. It should also be recognized that, when the filler neck extends to the bottom of the tank, refueling is much more difficult and the chance of fuel overflowing on the deck is increased with consequent increase in fire hazard. Experience with hundreds of thousands of boats and millions of automobiles fails to disclose any explosion hazard in the tank itself, and I wonder if it would not be safer all the way around to extend the filler neck just to the top of the tank.

"Records indicate that the majority of explosions take place upon starting the engine following a period of idleness. The operator touches the starter switch and the boat blows up. Three things are necessary of this explosion—a fuel leak, a proper mixture of air and fuel vapor and a source of ignition. It is doubtful if the ignition source can be eliminated entirely, and perhaps the most effective way of preventing these accidents is not to have any fuel in the bilge at all. One school of thought is to catch the fuel leaks after they occur and the other is to prevent fuel leaks by cutting off the fuel at the tank. From personal experience, I believe the two principal trouble spots as far as fuel leaks are concerned are the fuel lines and the carburetor, both of which deserve some rather careful attention. A drip pan under the carburetor is recommended at the present time. Unfortunately, the size of the drip pan is usually limited to not over a pint, and most fuel tanks are apt to be above the level of the carburetor. This is true especially with a gravity system. In the event of a leaking carburetor it is only a question of time before all or part of the contents of the fuel tank may leak through the carburetor, fill up the drip pan and then overflow into the bilge. Unless the drip pan is at least as large as the fuel tank, its value is somewhat limited and therefore questionable. Another common source of fuel leaks is in the fuel line near the engine. The carburetor drip pan is useless in this condition. Copper tubing is popular for fuel lines and has many advantages for this purpose although it has poor fatigue properties. Because all engines vibrate to a certain extent, a flexible fuel line next to the engine is very desirable and may eliminate most of the fuel leaks from this source. The aircraft industry, incidentally, dropped the use of metal tubing for fuel lines going to the engine and substituted the flexible fuel line some twenty years ago.

"Since the carburetor drip pan is no safeguard against fuel leaks from the carburetor and offers no help in the event of a leaking fuel line, it seems that the most effective method of coping with these trouble spots is cutting off the fuel at the tank every time the engine is stopped. If gasoline leaks in the bilge can be eliminated while the boat is idle, it changes the entire picture of drip pans, bilge blowers and so forth. A manual or automatic shutoff valve on the fuel line near the tank appears to be one of the most effective methods of overcoming fuel leaks in the bilge and gets at the source of trouble rather than attempting to catch the leaks after they occur. The shutoff valve, if manually operated, should be an improved packless type of valve with a handle extension which can be reached from some point on deck and not in the engine compartment. An automatic shutoff valve, either vacuum or electric, which shuts off the fuel every time the engine is stopped may be one of the most effective safety measures that can be investigated by this committee.

"Concerning some of the sources of ignition, I am inclined to discount backfires from carburetors inasmuch as practically all boats today have backfire traps, yet they still blow up and catch fire. Modern engines, furtherfore, unlike their ancestors of thirty years ago, seldom backfire. All of the indications seem to point to the engine ignition and electrical system as sources of ignition for these explosions. Anyone who has worked on engines, both new and old, realizes that the high tension ignition system has a miniature fireworks display inside the distributor cap. There is a virtual blaze of electrical discharges, and these caps, incidentally, are vented to the atmosphere. The high tension ignition wires frequently have electrical discharges on the outside, including the so-called "corona" effects, and there may be minute discharges over the spark plug insulators. Commutators on generators and open switches are also potential sources of ignition. It would be a difficult job to eliminate all of these electrical discharges, and the most effective method seems to be cutting off the fuel at the tank to eliminate any chance of fuel leaking into the bilge while the boat is idle.

"Since drip pans, backfire traps, bilge blowers and automatic fire extinguisher systems will not prevent an explosion following a period of idleness, I have been reluctant to feel these were the solution to the safety problem on my own boat, but I feel much safer when the fuel is cut off at the tank whenever the engine is stopped. . . .

"The present recommendations covering the prevention of fires and explosions on boats have certainly been beneficial in improving safety. However, explosions still take place even on boats complying with these recommendations. It is to be hoped that this conference will carry this work further and, in view of recent data, make the necessary additions and changes in order to bring about greater safety from the hazards of fires and explosions traceable to gasoline."

Mr. Murray's suggestion to cut off the fuel at the tank is one I heartily approve. Since 1927, or thereabouts, I have made it a practice in all my auxiliary designs, and in some power boat designs, to show the gasoline tank or tanks above the cockpit floor fitted with readily accessible shut-off valves also above the cockpit floor. I have also in my two books and in scores of magazine articles stressed the importance of shutting down an engine — NOT by turning off the ignition — but by shutting off the fuel supply and permitting the engine to run idle until the fuel in the supply line and carburetor is exhausted. If this is made standard practice there can be no fuel inside the boat to leak and find its way into the bilge. AND, consequently, no fires or explosions!

With proper attention given the openings in the cockpit floor through which the fuel lines run, and these are therefore water and gasoline tight, neither spillage nor leaks from the tanks can find their way below. This pre-supposes the cockpit floor is water tight and self-draining as it certainly should be.

The only difficulty I have found with this very safe and simple system of fuel supply is to convince owners of its worth and safety — and to find boat builders who will properly install it, the latter being the greater effort of the two.

*   *   *

Now, turning from methods of safety in the installation of gasoline and fuel oil tanks in power boats and auxiliaries, let's look into the pastime of going to sea for fun in small boats. Let's look backward a matter of forty years, or so — let's consider today — and let's look into the promises of tomorrow. The sea remains its own honest self, the boats which ply it are more frail than those of yesterday, but our collective attitude in connection with the wholesome fun of using it as a vast playground has completely changed, and I am afraid for the worse. There was a time; but read on, Shipmates.

Farther along in the pages of this book there is a refreshing account of the voyage of the 22 ft. water line sloop, *Gauntlet,* in the first race from New York to Bermuda, sponsored by Sir Thomas J. Lipton. This was written the year of the race, 1906, by Mr. Charles G. Davis who for more years than I can remember has been a prolific writer of things having to do with the sea; its boats, yachts and sailing ships. *Gauntlet* was designed and built the previous winter, I believe, by Mr. L. D. Huntington at New Rochelle, N. Y.

Built and rigged in the sound and ship-shape tradition of all Mr. Huntington's little cruising boats, *Gauntlet* had the unquestioned ability to poke her stout bows into bad weather and challenging seas with every prospect of besting the worst violence, "the more or less honest forces of nature", as William W. Nutting used to say, might throw in the way.

Since *Gauntlet's* day how the procedure of setting out to sea in cruising yachts has changed. Then, when once the land was left below the horizon, the little ship was on her own and her crew alone responsible for the navigation and safety of the vessel, the well-being of those aboard, and a safe arrival at her scheduled destination. If trouble came it was met by the resourcefulness and fortitude of the crew with the means at hand and the judgement of the master. At sea in those days one lived in a world completely detached from the land and, by the same token, in a freedom which, unfortunately, will never again bless the course of any of us. Such, I suppose, is the price we pay for the implements, inventions, contrivances, instruments, and complexities of present day living whether afloat or ashore.

In our day if one attempted to set sail in a small boat bound for ports beyond the horizon he would be considered as good as lost at sea by experts in the pastime of cruising and the sport of ocean-racing unless his little packet was *modestly* equipped with the new-day aids to navigation—radar, speedometer, telephone, fathometer, radio, automatic steering, and gyro compass. "Absolute necessities, these," my highly competitive minded ocean-racing friend, Comdr. Magellan Bowditch Mercator Hotstuff, says. "Absolute necessities, my dear fellow, suppose our spreader lights should fail to throw their soft glow over our decks? This would be disastrous. At a time like this a telephone to summon the Coast Guard for aid is vital. And how are we to know the time without a radio? Or how far we have travelled without a speedometer? The depth of water without a fathometer? Or for that matter, to see where we are going without radar? Absolute necessities, my dear fellow. And while the automatic steerer keeps us full-and-by we have time to listen to the baseball scores, stock market reports, our favorite news commentator, and the percentages in the latest Gallup poll. The automatic steerer also permits us time to view the accompanying fleet of Coast Guard and Navy vessels with their umbrella squadrons of autogyros and air-rescue planes — an inspiring sight, my dear friend, reminiscent of glorious days at Normandy, Anzio and the beach-heads at the Islands of the Pacific — an inspiring sight, indeed."

Thus, Shipmates, seems to be the channel of safety into which the experts of electrical and mechanical bewilderments are leading many cruising and racing yachtsmen who venture off-shore, or, for that matter, along shore. And, by the same measure, thus vanishes the independence, charm, and peace of close acquaintance with the moods of nature as these control the vastness of the sea, its calms, fair winds, tides, storms, life, and little ships.

And as for safety? Perhaps it might be as well to forsake the quest of this and turn the pages backward to wholesomeness of simplicity and the encouragement of cruising in genuine little ships of the sea — not the progeny of the scientists or the trailer-cradled frail craft which voyage over the highways for week-end rendezvous with competition and a few hours visit with the sea.

Spring
Fever

by C. G. Davis

MARY·ELLA
OF
SPEONK

BROAD BILL
OF
PATCHOGUE

EVANGELINE
FRIENDSHIP·ME.

FRESH PAINT

WHISTLE WING IV.
NOANK CONN.

Pendragon—"THRASHING GRANDLY DOWN THE BAY ON A BROAD REACH, HER HEADSAILS PULLING STRONGLY, TILLER ALIVE, BUT DOCILE AS ALWAYS".

From a drawing
by Theodore Ewen

Pendragon

W. C. Godard

L EAN back against the bulkhead and join me in my day-dream. I'm
leafing through a sheaf of papers, letters, lists and bills, from designer's correspondence to registry papers.

Here we have a letterhead William Atkin — Naval Architect,
". . . by now you must have the plans." Yes, I had them and was deep
in the fascinating business of making hardware lists and figuring costs.
She was a beauty, even on paper. A double ended hull, ketch rigged,
gaff headed on both main and mizzen to permit of lower, solid spars
with attendant economy; raised deck construction 'midships, with well
deck forward to help in handling ground tackle and headsails. Neat,
practical, with a definite salty touch. Dimensions 34 ft. 7 in. by 30 ft.
by 10 ft. 4 in. by 4 ft. 10 in. with 21,000 pounds displacement.

Now Gearge E. Richardson and Son, Boatbuilders of Richardson,
Deer Island—many of these. A good, honest builder, and a wondrous
patient one! I see again the big rambling shed and rigging loft, with
steam rotary nearby; cold, clean Bay of Fundy tidewater over the launching ways. The fitting out berth and the office, with its walls lined with
models of today and yesteryear. What a place to visit! How desperate-
ly hard to leave.

Letters with little problems such as; knightheads or the *Norse* turn-
down on her rail forward (we stood out for the old world touch),
canvas turned under guards or let into rabbet in the covering board (we
adopted the latter and were greatly pleased over the years), galley bulkhead as shown, or dropped (we lowered it for better circulation of air
and effect of space), eye-bolts and rod instead of pintles on the big
rudder (we tried that too, with satisfaction). And letters with larger
problems as well, such as, ". . . will have to have a stick of white oak
24 ft. by 22 in. by 8 in., as none of the logs you brought will give us
what we need."

Of course he got it. Here is the bill-of-lading from Eastern Canada
Coastal Steamships, destination Deer Island.

But I am guilty of an anachronism. Those oak logs—yes, here's
the receipt from Farmer Wilkins, 1,000 ft. white oak logs. Nearer
1,500 ft., it was, as that fine gentleman scaled only to the first sweep
in a log.

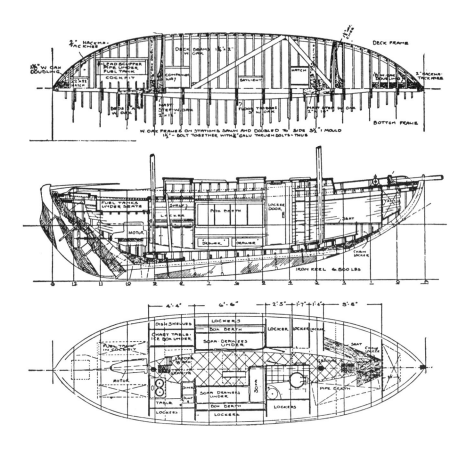

MR. GODARD'S GAFF HEAD KETCH *Pendragon* IS 34 FT. 7 IN. OVERALL;
30 FT. ON THE DESIGNED WATERLINE; 10 FT. 4 IN. IN BREADTH AND HAS
A MODEST DRAFT OF 4 FT. 10 IN. HER TOTAL SAIL AREA OF 582 SQ. FT. IS
DIVIDED INTO FOUR WORKING SAILS WITH 270 SQ. FT. IN THE MAIN, 116
SQ. FT. IN THE MIZZEN, 90 SQ. FT. IN THE STAYSAIL AND 106 SQ. FT. IN
THE JIB. THE MAIN AND MIZZEN, BEING GAFF-HEADED, ARE IN KEEPING
WITH HER SEA-KINDLY HULL. *Pendragon's* CONSTRUCTION DRAWING,
REPRODUCED ABOVE, SHOWS THE DECK AND BOTTOM FRAMING PLANS
COMBINED WITH THE INBOARD PROFILE AND INTERIOR ARRANGEMENT
PLAN. BELOW DECK SHE IS LAID OUT FOR THE COMFORTABLE ACCOM-
MODATION FOR A PARTY OF THREE, IF SHORT CRUISES ARE CONTEM-
PLATED, BUT FOR TWO IF A LONG VOYAGE OR LIVING ABOARD IS
PLANNED.

122

Now a receipt from the Transport Company. "One load logs Coles Island to Deer Island". Much more here than meets the eye. A brisk mid-November morning, two men and I in a stake body truck equipped with extra low gear, bouncing along before daybreak bound from Saint John out along the Kennebecassis River valley, over Keirstead Mountain to Coles Island and a stack of racked oak logs. Then the muscle-straining loading, and off again after lunch. A long grind in double low up the mountain and a glorious rush down the other side. The debate as to whether, in the event of a sudden stop, the load would, or would not, shear the cab from the truck. The hair-raising sight of two buggies jogging along abreast down the middle of the road, drivers swapping yarns! Our frantic horn and smoking brakes, the slow parting of the gossips as our juggernaut roared between. No decision in the argument.

We didn't make it that day. Forty miles short of the L'tete Ferry that long-suffering truck refused duty. We jacked the load off the tires and went home to let her cool off. Next morning early—very early— as we suspected by now that our load was considerably in excess of highway weight restrictions, we again got underway and reached the ferry in good order. The operator cast his experienced eye over our load and opined, "Can't do it, son. Have to take her by special trip and charge you accordin' . . ." The oak of course must go through. "How much?" "Set price, son, can't do no better; that'll be 75¢". Anticlimax! How good it sounded finally to hear those logs catapult off into the builder's yard as we cut the restraining cinch lines.

More letters follow, ordering hardware from that very satisfactory firm, Laughlin of Portland, inquiring as to motors, pricing sailcloth, paints, etcetera. Slowly the dates advance through an interminable winter.

At length the month of May and the ferry back in service. I quote from this one. It was pure music to my ears. "I am sending you a ferry time table. We have the yacht all planked, caulked, the ballast in and we will finish ceiling tomorrow, so if you want to see her under construction you had better come down quick!"

So the trip to the Island is made again. No stimulus of bill-head, letter or printed word is needed to recapture the thrill of opening the boat shed door that May morning and seeing at long last the hull that had occupied our thoughts all winter. My wife, unused to the loom and bulk of a boat under cover, gasped out at me, "Man, are you crazy?"

The boat did indeed appear immense, but assumed her proper personality and proportions with a few miles of open water about her. How able those 1½ in. by 3½ in. frames looked when in place. How satisfying, the 1¼ in. planking. As I remember there was little or nothing to cavil at and much, very much to commend and admire. Truly there is no substitute for experience, and George E. Richardson, a man over eighty, had been a boat builder all his days.

Then the last letter. Not a Chaucer nor a Ruskin had this man's mastery of prose, ". . . a few lines to let you know we put the *Pendragon* in this afternoon. Washed her face with sea water. Helen did the job. She went okay."

The rigging, splicing and reeving off, lacing on of her canvas, motor tune up and trials I will pass over. Hard work and time consuming, but a labour of love. She proved wonderfully satisfactory to handle and to live aboard. Tight alow and aloft, we kept our quart milk supply in her bilge sump and never had to explain that "skylights always weep a bit". Of her performance I do not consider myself a competent judge—she did everything we asked of her, and did it well. Suffice it to say we felt no twinge of envy in any company.

My wish is that you too could see the finished yacht as my mind's eye conjures her up. At anchor, perchance in one of our northern spruce clad coves, her rode perpendicular in the black water, spars etched against the last of the sunset, a plume of woodsmoke above her Charlie Noble—or thrashing grandly down the Bay on a broad reach, her headsails pulling strongly, tiller alive, but docile as always. And I wonder, along with Omar, as I turn over the last receipt and voucher, what little money buys these skilled brains and clever hands, one-half so precious as the things they sell!

Katydidn't

In God we trust-
all others cash

William W. Atkin

THE makings of a happy life seem to stem from a series of happy
incidents and from knowing people who are right for you. My life
is no exception. It has been, so far, a singularly happy one. Having
Billy Atkin for a father, his wife for a mother and his son for a brother
apparently got me off on the right foot.

But the thing my father asked me to tell about for THE SECOND
BOOK OF BOATS, is a series of incidents in my life which had to do
with boats, and, incidentally, with some of the wonderful people who
make up the boating fraternity.

There was a rubbish heap in South Norwalk, Connecticut, and
over it ran a runway to a decrepit old building that had a long history
as a boat shop. The boats that were produced there were large, sturdy
rowing boats of the type beloved by clammers and fishermen. It would
be impossible for me to estimate how many of these boats were built

in the shop and it is difficult to remember how much they sold for. My impression is it was somewhere in the neighborhood of $10.00 apiece. That was in the days, not so far removed either, when prices were somewhat different from what they are now.

The man who built all these wonderful boats was Captain Joe Fowler. The shop he built them in was always known as Captain Joe Fowler's Boat Shop—a very logical name. Besides the old building overlooking Norwalk Harbor, where the rowboats were built, there was a yard. Captain Joe always hauled up a few small boats for winter storage in the yard. Sometimes, he had a major or minor repair job to do for someone and the first time I saw the place was when a friend took me there to look at an old boat he had salvaged and Captain Joe was repairing for him. The boat was a 16 foot yawl-boat from a three-masted lumber schooner and the young man who owned it was Gerry Colmore.

Gerry was a boy, really, and he loved boats, particularly old boats. So when he saw the yawl-boat, badly battered, on the beach in Old Greenwich, he felt sorry for her. He spoke of all boats as though they were humans and he felt as bad about seeing this little hooker going to pieces on the beach as he would have felt if he saw an old woman, badly beaten, lying on the sidewalk or in the gutter. It was imperative that something be done and since larger boat shops charged more for their work than Gerry could afford to pay, he took the boat to Joe Fowler. But there was another advantage to taking her to Joe Fowler's shop. Joe understood this kind of a boat better than the man in the average yacht yard. Captain Joe refitted the little yawl-boat but Gerry never had a chance to sail her because war was brewing in Europe and Gerry, being an Englishman, went to England in 1937 and joined the Royal Air Force. But my father has told the story in MOTOR BOATING much more eloquently than I can tell it. In this he named a boat in memory of Gerry—a fine 33 foot stem head sloop. Here is what my father has to say about that name—Gerry Colmore.

"The name? Well Shipmates, in lasting memory of a young man, a very young man my sons liked, and we liked. A young man whose love centered on an old Friendship sloop, the *Irving D. Olson,* built years ago by Charles Morse of Down East fame. Born of British army folks, Gerry's family thought it best for him to live in tradition befitting an army man's son and not in the inclination that led him to happiness and the fragrancies of American yacht harbors, boat yards, and the snug cabin of the *Irving D. Olson*. And so one day a year or so ago (1937) Gerry sailed for England to become a flying officer in the beloved army of his forbears. And all too soon after, a telegram came. 'In the performance of duty', it read, 'Cadet Gerald Fellowes Colmore was killed in an air crash this morning.' Not yet twenty, shipmates. How much better the indolence, the fragrancy, the snug cabin of the *Irving D. Olson?*"

Tradition has it that when a sailing man dies he finds Valhalla. If this is so, both Gerry and Joe Fowler are there now. You can be sure, too, that they will not be found at a swank Valhalla Yacht club for they are navigation-wise and will scull their boats across the River Jordan to a corner reserved for cruising men, honest boat builders, lobstermen, fishermen and other sterling saltwater-soaked lovers of the sea.

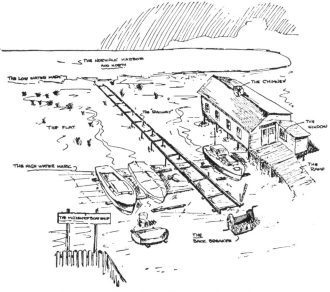

THE MIZZEN TOP BOAT SHOP—AT THE HEAD OF A LONG MUD FLAT— BUILDERS OF THE LITTLE PRAM *Katydidn't*.

All of this leads up to my connection with Joe Fowler's Boat Shop. When first I visited there with Gerry Colmore I had no idea that one day it would be my own boat shop. It was, though, and it provided, besides a living of sorts, a year filled with interesting and amusing incidents that fit into the category of never-to-be-forgotten events.

It is not quite accurate to say that the shop was mine for I had a partner, and without him I would never have tackled the venture. His name is Art Javes. He had been bitten by the boating bug several years before I met him, and had built a boat in his backyard. At that time he was working in a lace mill, of all places. For all we know, if he hadn't built that first boat, he might still be tatting, warping, woofing and whatever else is done in a lace mill. But he was hit hard and nothing would satisfy him but to become a good boat builder. For Art this seemed to be rather easy to do because, while his apprenticeship was short, he is now an expert boat builder and has learned designing as well. We rented the shop from Joe Fowler's widow for $10.00 a month. Along with the shop we had the privilege of using the yard for storage. In honor of the old Atkin homestead in Huntington, L. I., we called our shop the Mizzen Top Boat Shop. My first job, on taking possession, was to paint a sign to put at the end of the street so that prospective customers would be able to find the shop.

The shop and yard were at the head of a long mud flat. At high water we never had more than four feet of water at the bottom of the "railway". Like everything else about the Mizzen Top, the railway was unusual. It consisted of some heavy timbers imbedded in the mud. When we wanted to haul a boat, all we had to do was to grease the timbers with tallow, dive into the water and nail braces under the boat to be hauled, and start hauling. Art and I always felt a little silly about the winch at the Mizzen Top because it took two of us to operate it. I have often thought that Joe Fowler must have been a very muscular man because at 60 or 70 he, presumably, just turned that crank as though he were turning a coffee grinder. We, on the other hand, found it extremely tough to turn. After about twenty backbreaking cranks we would find the boat we were hauling had moved, perhaps, two feet up the railway. After several hours of sweating, and resting, we would manage to get a boat up to the point where it could be moved for storage.

Another feature of the shop was the rubbish pile under the ramp which led to the shop. This mass of debris attracted something like twenty or thirty cats. These were not of the friendly, domesticated variety, but wild cats. The feline has never attracted me much at best and if I needed anything to persuade me that cats are not nice animals, my experience at the Mizzen Top did the job. I must confess that the cats did not bother me particularly; they seemed quite self-sufficient in their home among the clam shells, paper boxes, old tin cans and other rubbish under the ramp. One day however, I think Art and I bothered them. For as long as Captain Joe had the shop, he had put up with a chimney right in the middle of the building floor. We felt we would accomplish a more spacious effect if we removed the chimney and put a metal stovepipe out the window. We asked Mrs. Fowler if she had any objections to our removing the chimney and she told us that she didn't. However, she did ask us to be careful because she didn't want us to put any holes in the roof or the floor. Now Art Javes is a man who believes in direct action. His motto is to get a job done as fast as possible. So our method for taking the chimney down was a little faster than it was safe. We knocked out a row of bricks, with the exception of two in diagonally opposite corners, from around the bottom of the chimney. Then, with two sledges, Art on one corner and I on the other, knocked out the last two bricks and ran like hell. The crash that followed could be heard for miles and neighbors converged on the shop from all sides. Mrs. Fowler, who had been sitting in the dining room of her house looking out at the shop, saw the chimney sticking through

"... AND THIRTY-ODD CATS WERE SEEN SCAMPERING IN ALL DIRECTIONS AWAY FROM THE SHOP".

the roof one second and a gaping hole the next. Split seconds after this tremendous crash, great howlings arose from under the ramp and thirty-odd cats were seen scampering in all directions away from the shop.

At the end of the boat shop, the inland end, Captain Joe had built a privy—a two-holer. The privy was located on the south side of the ramp that led into the shop. When Art and I took over we found the privy dark and dreary. We felt that we could improve it immeasurably by installing a large window in one side. On one of Art's days off I decided to install the window and get that chore out of the way. I did the work in rather short order, I thought, and the window sash fit the hole I cut for it very beautifully indeed.

I built a partition and installed shelves for storage on one side leaving the other side for its original purpose. The next day when Art arrived I proudly showed him my work of the previous day expecting him to enthuse over my skill (which is not at all great). Instead, he said, "My God, Willie, you got it backwards". I inspected the sash and found, to my delight, that he was wrong. My triumph did not last long, though, because it turned out that what he meant was I had put the window in the wrong side of the privy. If I'd put the window on the south side, it would have overlooked the mud flat and the occupant would have had complete privacy and everything would have been acceptable. But I had the window on the north side in full view of every person who walked down the ramp toward the shop. We had a problem there but we decided it would be a lot of unnecessary work to change the window to the other side and so we tried to devise a means of getting privacy for the occupant of the privy without changing the window location.

We discussed the possibility of curtains at the window but quickly dismissed the idea as out of place in a boat shop. As we were bemoaning our fate and trying to decide how long it would take to change the window, Art had an inspiring thought. All we had to do, Art said, was to work out a plan to divert the customer's attention from the window. Immediately we became actors. I played the double role of occupant of the privy and approaching customer while Art played the role of official Mizzen Top greeter. As the customer, I walked down the ramp toward the door. Art, standing inside and playing "Chickee" for Atkin, the privy occupant, immediately rushed out of the shop door and greeted Atkin, the customer, quite effusively. As we walked down the ramp, he subtly edged me around by pointing out an imaginary boat that was hauled up in the yard, so that my back was toward the window. Once he had gotten me in the door, all was well and Atkin, the privy occupant, had no further fear of shocking the modesty of the customer. It always seemed a pity to me that we never had a chance to try out the technique in a real situation but, as luck would have it, our customers always arrived at more opportune moments.

The only boat we ever built was a pram dinghy, *Katydidn't,* and a wonderful little boat she is. Her length is 6 ft. 6 in, breadth 3 ft. 4 in. and depth, 1 ft. 1½ in.

If it weren't for a patient little girl named Helen, I doubt that this boat ever would have been finished for it was she who spent hours and hours sandpapering the inside of the boat. We discovered that sandpaper has about the same effect on Casco glue, once it has set, as it does on steel, so after we had put on several of the strips we wiped off the glue that squeezed out of the seams with a slightly dampened cloth and this solved the problem.

THE ROUND BOTTOM PRAM *Katydidn't*
UNDER CONSTRUCTION.

Katydidn't is so light she can be very easily carried by one man; so tight that lying upside down in the summer's sun has no effect on her watertightness. She rows well with two passengers and can carry three. Indicative of the worth of edge-nailed (or strip) planking is the fact that, although this boat has been stored for eight years on the rafters under our garage roof, she could be put into the water tomorrow and after one sponging would remain dry. A number of people who have stopped in my father's office have wanted to buy *Katydidn't* but he will not sell her. He is saving this remarkable little boat for the day when he builds his new cruising boat.

I suppose the boat building business is a precarious one in the best times but when Art and I ran the Mizzen Top, the times left much to be desired. Both of us had to find more lucrative work, Art, because he was going to get married, I, because I knew that I would never be a good boatbuilder and if Art left I'd never find a partner to take his place. Thus, the Mizzen Top Boat Shop has passed into limbo. The story wouldn't be complete, though, unless I told you about the wedding.

Art worked at the shop toward the end only on days when it rained. Other days he had a job that he could do only on sunny, clear days. When he and Helen, our sandpaperer, decided to get married, the financial situation was at its grimmest and Art prayed daily for sunshine. They went to get the marriage license and arrange for blood tests on a rainy day. According to Connecticut law, the blood test is good for 33 days and since the cumulative total for Helen and Art was $10.00, it was essential that they be married within the 33 days limit so they wouldn't have to dig up another $10.00 for repeat blood tests. Thirty-two of the thirty-three days passed with the sun shining gloriously and Art and Helen decided that they would get married on the last day sun or super sun. Of course it rained so Helen married Art and they will live happily ever after. Me? Oh, I was in love too. And she got married, but not to me.

Just inside the door of the Mizzen Top Boat Shop hung a large sign; In God we trust — all others cash. This always amused me, hence, the title for Bill's story.

The three accompanying scratch board illustrations were drawn by Kevin Royt.

Mr. Cleat

A small cruising ketch

Thomas C. Gillmer

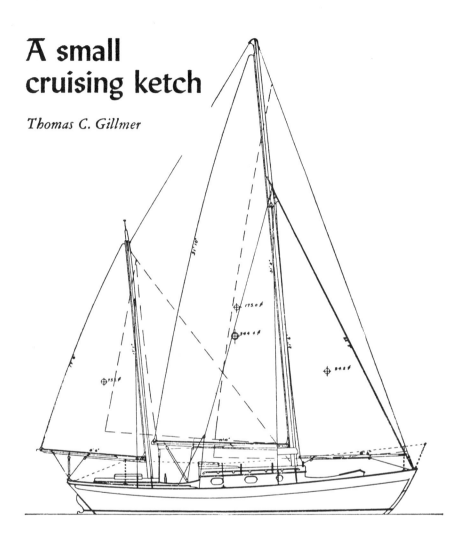

TOO many prospective boatmen demand a small boat with big boat performance. This is too bad because it is generally inexperience and confusion of facts which lead to such an unreasonable demand and consequently the boating world is cheated of another devotee. On the other hand a man who has acquired some experience with boats and has become mellowed in his demands by ownership of boats will see the folly of expecting too much. He has realized that the cruising

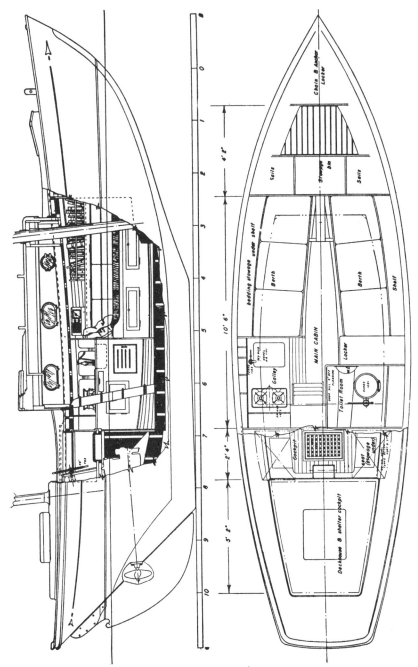

FULL HEADROOM, ADEQUATE STORAGE AND A LARGE ENCLOSED TOILET ROOM ARE INCLUDED IN THE CONVENIENT LAYOUT.

limits of a boat are almost directly proportional (other characteristics being equal) to its size or displacement. There still remains a healthy urge however, to own a boat of able performance and seaworthy character; on the rugged side. One that is not too costly to build nor too large to be handled and kept up by one man. Such a desire is quite reasonable.

Herewith is presented a design of such a boat. The conventional ketch rig was decided upon for several reasons. In the first place the sail area is broken into increments that will not by themselves be too great a handful. Secondly these smaller increments may be used in combination to shorten the sail area without the awkwardness of reefing. Replacement and repair of damaged sails are less costly, as well.

The principal dimensions of this little ketch are: 29 ft. overall, 24 ft. on the waterline, 8 ft. 2 in. beam and 4 ft. draft. Her displacement is just under 11,000 lbs. As constructed she is rugged but within the limits of easily flowing lines. She has a rather fine entrance with a flat run aft under her counter. Her bilges are moderately hard combining with sections that develop strong, natural stability characteristics.

Her layout includes a main cabin with full headroom throughout, with the conventional two berths, galley, toilet room and adequate stowage with hanging locker. There is a sort of shelter cabin-cockpit aft separated from the main cabin by a regular cockpit. This after cabin arrangement has been suggested by several deep water cruising authorities who prefer such arrangement to the wasted space of a large open cockpit aft. There is little to recommend it for afternoon or weekend sailing but for longer cruising and open water work it should be most useful, in its additional bulk stowage space, extra hand berthing or merely as a sheltered steering station.

One feature in construction of the cabin top will be noticeable in the absence of the usual cabin beams. These have been omitted to gain a clear and unobstructed overhead. The construction is edge fastened, strip planking with two auxiliary spans on the exterior serving doubly as dinghy skids.

The rig is all inboard with provision for light sails including mizzen staysail. The total working sail area is 345 sq. ft. The standing rigging and halyards are of stainless steel.

She is amply powered with a small (12 HP) two cylinder engine. This auxiliary may appear on the lighter side, it is intended though to be true auxiliary power, of excellent economy, thus giving better cruis-

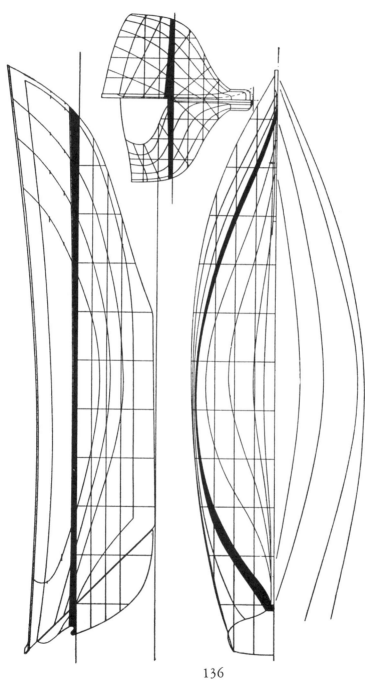

THE PRINCIPAL DIMENSIONS OF MR. GILLMER'S KETCH RIGGED AUXILIARY ARE: 29 FT. OVERALL, 24 FT. ON THE WATERLINE, 8 FT. 2 IN. BEAM AND 4 FT. DRAFT. HER LINES, AS REPRODUCED ABOVE, GIVE INDICATION OF TIME WELL SPENT IN THEIR DEVELOPMENT. HER COUNTER STERN IS PLEASINGLY SHAPED.

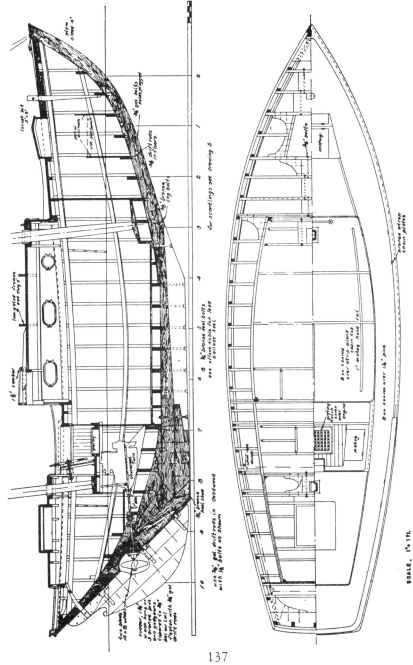

SCALE, 1" = 1ft.

THE CONSTRUCTION PLAN IS ALSO INDICATIVE OF CARE AND CONSIDERATION IN DETERMINING VARIOUS COMPONENTS.

137

ing radius under power than heavier engines which will hardly gain a knot more speed. The tank capacity should give a 600 mile cruising radius under power.

The inference may be strong that this boat is suitable for off shore use. No designer should be asked to commit himself on this sort of question. The suitability of this type of boat to extensive offshore cruising is a question for the owner to decide. The designer can, of course, provide that the boat is adequate in stability, strength and performance but such items as comfort and stowage are large considerations to successful offshore cruising. These latter are functions of volume. Suffice it is to say that most any small, strongly built and well modeled boat can cruise off shore. There is little more chance of foundering or swamping than her much larger sisters. She will take it comfortably far longer and to a greater extent than can those aboard her.

Possibly brief comment by your editors on Mr. Gillmer's
ketch will not be amiss.
When we first saw the plans of his boat we were delighted.
And the more we looked over her plans the more delighted we
became.
She embodies a great many of the qualities required in a
wholesome cruising boat. As Mr. Gillmer has written, her sail
area is broken up into comparatively small units. With this
arrangement the boat will remain in balance under a number of
combinations of sails.
The arrangement of the cockpit, trunk cabin and the wide
waterways is most practical. Steering from just abaft amidships
will provide many advantages. Among these will be less motion
in a seaway, a far more secure position, better visibility both
under power and sail and, incidentally, the creation of a large
lazerette for stowage of all the gear required on a small boat
going to sea.
The lines show a boat with firm bilges and nice flare forward,
both of which will tend to keep the boat stable and dry.
She has a particularly pleasing sheerline and this gives the boat
a ship-shape appearance all the way 'round.
All in all, we are very glad to say, Mr. Gillmer has
produced a very handsome little boat and one that will prove
an excellent sea-goer as well as one having that difficult-to-
obtain qualification "character."

Mr. Ratline

schooner
STEPHEN TABER
Capt. Guild

QUEEN OF THE COASTERS

From a drawing by Mr. Cornelius Van Ness

The centerboard coasting schooner
Stephen Taber was built at Glenwood, N.Y.
in 1871. She is now owned by Captain Frederick
B. Guild and sails out of Boothbay Harbor, Maine. The
Taber is 70 ft. overall and, tho of greater dimensions than boats
generally featured in the BOOK OF BOATS, is of interest as a "boat of
yesterday—going strong today".

Store of information

Conducted by the
Messrs. Cleat, Garboard and Ratline

A RELATIVELY large number of letters have come along in connection with this STORE OF INFORMA-TION — letters suggesting our increasing the scope of the STORE, which we are doing; letters commenting on the authoritive nature of the information presented; and even <u>one</u> letter from a doctor Down East 'way who prepared stew in strict accordance with Abel Brown's famed recipe, which appeared in the STORE of the FIRST BOOK. And to make this feat more intriquing the doctor prepared the stew while <u>actually</u> aboard a "brilliantly planning" hull. His only comment was that Abel Brown is to be highly complimented for concocting a recipe so <u>utterly simple</u>!!

cantilever top

"-and with an aspect ratio of plane of only .4662 this hull is planing at a modest 48 m.p.h. with a class B model airplane engine."

The above sketch, made from an actual drawing, clearly shows the superior, level-riding qualities of these super-sonic hulls. Steam, from the cooking stew, is <u>streaming</u> from the Liverpool head.

Again we have gathered together a group of recipes, procedures, rudiments, discussions, instructions and interesting anecdotes to make up this STORE OF INFORMATION. These are compiled from the experience of cruising friends; our own experience; from other reliable sources and now including material received from readers of the FIRST BOOK.

This STORE is to continue in future issues and will be made far more interesting, valuable and entertaining by actual experiences submitted by our readers.

A letter from H.R.P., of San Diego, California has suggested methods of preventing inside iron ballast from rusting. He mentions that, "nothing is much more annoying than having the bilges dirty from the red rust of inside ballast." And this is surely true.

Conducting experiments with various pieces of iron, he determined that the old-time mixture of one gallon of spirits of turpentine, 1 lb. 4 oz. of rosin, 1 lb. 4 oz. of lampblack and 1 qt. of linseed oil mixed together and boiled slowly for half an hour was the most satisfactory coating to prevent rust.

This mixture is actually black varnish and will be found useful in numerous ways around a boat.

An easier method, tho not quite as effective, is to whitewash the ballast with hot lime.

Another excellent protection for iron ballast is a coating of cement and water (grout)

This method was used on the ballast of the little Friendship sloop *Great Republic* and proved entirely satisfactory for many years. And the old stand-bys white and red leads do an excellent job in preventing rust from forming. After carefully chipping excess rust and scale from the ballast and two coats of red lead are applied there will be little rust accumulated thru the summer months.

 One gallon of paint will cover 450 sq. ft. of wood and 720 sq. ft. of smooth iron plate. Average paint will dry in from six to eight hours and will be hard enough to walk on in about 24 hours ⇥ this depending on the analysis of the paint ⇥ a glossy paint, containing a large percentage of linseed oil will, for example, take longer to dry than a flat paint containing a larger percentage of turpentine. All paints will take longer to dry on iron or steel than on wood or semi-porous surfaces.

The problem of bleaching decks, which have become oil-stained, built up with old varnish or otherwise unattractive may be solved in a comparitively simple manner. However, precautions must be taken to prevent any of the following solutions from running out the scuppers and down the topsides, as they will undoubtedly have a deleterious effect on the painted surfaces. We suggest making white pine plugs to insert in the scuppers, making sure they are water tight before applying the following solution. Boil 6 lbs. American potash (potassium carbonate) in 1 gal. of clear water. Test the resulting solution by applying some to a piece of pine. If too strong it will turn the pine red and in this case add sufficient water until it does not affect the pine. Lay on the decks evenly, after sunset, and let it remain overnight, but do not allow it to harden. Before the sun rises, remove the plugs from the scuppers, and flush off the solution with <u>lots</u> of water and thoro scrubbing. Then scour the decks with sand, rubbed with holystone, which will remove all dirt, grease and varnish. Flush off well and take care to rinse off topsides, or any part of the deck which does not require treatment. When decks have thoroly dried apply a solution of one pound oxalic acid in one gallon of hot water ↝ and when this is washed off, the decks will be as white as snow.

Col. Dick Birnn has written, "I have experimented about half a dozen times with oil to keep wave tops down where they belong. Many yachtsmen advise using oil thru the toilet, giving it a pump now and then. However I have found it more easily used thru the galley sink ↝ just putting a small bundle of oil soaked rags in the sink and letting it drain out slowly. One time I controlled the flow very nicely by forcing a finishing nail alongside the rubber drain stopper, which gave just enough of an aperture to allow the oil to flow thru at the desired rate.

"One squally day, on the lower Chesapeake, I used some rancid cooking oil and let my boat drift downwind as the oil drained thru the sink discharge. That pint of oil certainly spread a huge, unruffled patch on the water, and tho the swells heaved us up and down, the wave tops were definitely <u>not</u> whipping loose and blowing horizontally against our boat.

"Another wintery day on Long Island Sound, when my late father-in-law's open motor boat broke down, we had to spend an hour cutting a new keyway in the propeller shaft at the coupling. We found that oil was a Godsend. It was bad enough to do this job in a heavy seaway ty but in the bitter cold, with the wind-blown spume, which froze as it hit, made things worse. Diluting some spare engine oil with gasoline, or rather thickening the gasoline with engine oil, we doused a badly torn kapok cushion with the mixture and secured it to an iron bucket making a crude sea anchor with oil bag. It worked well and we at least remained dry and ice-free while we worked. While the mixture we used was thin, it was just right for the low temperature.

The length of a nautical mile is defined as $\frac{1}{60}^{th}$ of a degree of a great circle of the earth. If the earth were a perfect sphere of known dimensions, the length of a nautical mile, according to the above definition, would be a definite and invariable quality. Owing, however, to the earth's compressions, and the consequent difference in the lengths of radii of curvature

144

at different points of its surface, much diversity has arisen in usage and in books of reference in assigning the lengths of a nautical mile. Thus it is variously given as equal to the mean length of a minute of latitude on the meridian, the length of a minute of the meridian corresponding to the radius of the equator ⅍ the latter definition being probably due to the common use among mariners of Mercator's projection, in which the degrees of the successive parallels of latitude are equal to those on the equator.

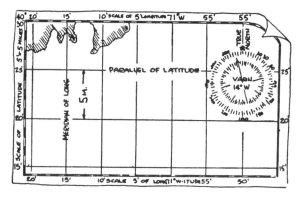

On Mercator charts, as above, of large areas, this scale varies as one moves up or down the chart, altho minutes of latitude always represent miles of distance in that latitude.

The office of the United States Coast Survey, in order to remove uncertainty, and to introduce uniformity, has adopted the value which results from considering the nautical mile as equal to the one-sixtieth part of the length of a degree on the great circle of a sphere whose surface is equal to the surface of the earth. This value, computed on Clark's spheroid, is:

ONE NAUTICAL MILE = 1853.248 metres ⅍
ONE NAUTICAL MILE = 6080.27 feet ⅍

The geographical mile and the sea mile are the same as the nautical mile or knot. The statute mile of America is 5,280 feet. ⅍

KNOTS		MILES		KNOTS		MILES
1	=	1.152		4	=	4.606
1¼	=	1.439		5	=	5.757
1½	=	1.727		6	=	6.909
1¾	=	2.015		7	=	8.061
2	=	2.303		8	=	9.212
2½	=	2.879		9	=	10.364
3	=	3.455		10	=	11.515

CONVERSELY:

MILES		KNOTS		MILES		KNOTS
1	=	0.868		4	=	3.474
1¼	=	1.086		5	=	4.342
1½	=	1.303		6	=	5.211
1¾	=	1.520		7	=	6.079
2	=	1.737		8	=	6.947
2½	=	2.171		9	=	7.816
3	=	2.605		10	=	8.684

Made fast on rail fitting ⅍ port or starboard ⅍

Dial indicates distance run.

50 to 100 ft. of braided log line.

rotator (actuates indicator on rail.)

TYPICAL TAFFRAIL or PATENT LOG

Run over known distance to check error ⅍ Length of line is important ⅍ If rotator skips line may be too short ⅍ Watch out for seaweed fouling rotator ⅍

146

The art of caulking boats may appear, to the un-initiated, nothing more than inserting cotton in the seams of a hull and pounding it in securely.

Actually there are few operations, if any, in the construction of a boat that is ladened with more potential dangers than a caulked seam. The same dangers apply in old or new boats. Caulking is not, therefore, a job that should be undertaken by the inexperienced as it is quite an art by itself and one that has a number of different methods of procedure. Summarized in a few words ↝ caulking should be driven <u>hard</u> into good seams and <u>easily</u> into poor seams and it should be remembered that caulking should be driven firmly into all seams.

Here is a caulker at work. He is in the process of hitting the mallet with an "underhand" stroke which is common. As a matter of fact the only time an "overhand" stroke is used is in caulking decks.

This caulking business hinges on numerous con-ditions for a good caulked seam depends, first, on good seams and good seams depend on good frames, sturdy fastenings and the correct beveling of the plank edges. The frames must be sufficiently strong to prevent the hull from moving about, or rather keep the planks from moving across the surface of the frames. Therefore the fastenings <u>must</u> be strong enough to "stay put". The term "nail sickness"

147

applies to fastenings which have lost their power of holding, have corroded, or are loose in the planking. And the term "cotton spitting" may be defined as an allied ill of "nailsickness".

Possibly the most important operation in planking a new boat is in seeing that all the planks have approximately the same width of seam and that the planks are provided with suitable outgage, or bevel, and that the inside of the seams fit tightly together.

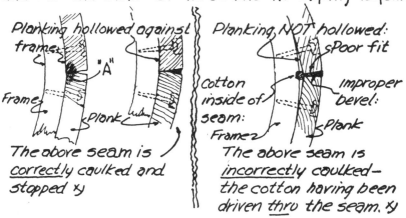

Planking hollowed against frames:
"A"
Frame
Plank
The above seam is correctly caulked and stopped xy

Planking, NOT hollowed:
Poor fit
Improper bevel:
Cotton inside of seam:
Frame
Plank
The above seam is incorrectly caulked— the cotton having been driven thru the seam. xy

This outgage shall be cut on the planks as shown, and does not, or should not, include the total thickness of the plank. There is indicated, by the shaded area "A", the portion of the planks, and seam, which takes the pressure of the caulking iron and the force exerted from the mallet blows. If the mallet blows are not carefully measured there will be a great chance of driving the caulking clear thru the seam which creates a "botch" job of the first degree and raises the possibility of splitting the inside edges of the seam. If, on occasion, the seams do not butt snugly and the cotton may be driven thru the seams, a batten should be screw fastened inside the planking prior to

148

any caulking being done.

The outgage, previously mentioned, is shown in the sketch of a "correctly caulked seam". The horizontal portion of the planking will allow the two planks to swell and make a tight seam without entirely depending on the caulking.

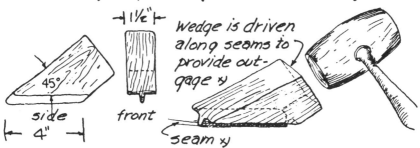

wedge is driven along seams to provide out-gage ×

← 1½" →

front

side

45°

← 4" →

seam ×

Seam wedge of locust or other hard wood

A seam wedge, as illustrated, is driven along, between planks to make the proper width and bevel on each seam. The depth of the fin is determined by the thickness of the planking used. This tool also bruises the plank edges slightly and causes the wood to swell easier.

It is essential that the caulked seam be painted immediately after being caulked. The application of this paint causes a slight swelling of both planking and cotton which, assisted by the film of paint as it dries, prevents the caulking from coming out or creeping. The practise of painting the seams with thin paint before caulking is a point for arquement and is not considered essential by some yards.

If a seam is very wide it should not simply be caulked with a single strand of cotton. By twisting a single strand the seam may be completely filled. If however, the seam is not filled by this twisting, it must be doubled back on itself. The wider the seam

149

the nearer together the twists. Using such a method the seams can be caulked uniformly.

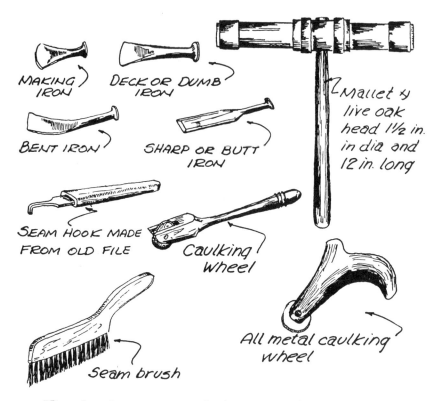

MAKING IRON

DECK OR DUMB IRON

BENT IRON

SHARP OR BUTT IRON

Mallet of live oak head 1½ in. in dia and 12 in. long

SEAM HOOK MADE FROM OLD FILE

Caulking Wheel

All metal caulking wheel

Seam brush

The tools required for caulking consist of a number of different irons. A mallet, particularly designed for caulking is manufactured and should be used rather than an iron headed hammer. An old file, bent over and fixed with a simple handle makes a fine tool for raking out old cotton. Seam brush is used to clean seams and to apply paint to the caulked seam. The caulking wheel has its disadvantage in that it sometimes runs off the seam and cuts a deep groove off at an angle. It is primarily used on light planking, bottoms of skiffs and similar

150

boats. The all metal caulking wheel is simply another version of wheel, with a cast iron handle and brass wheel.

In recaulking a boat, a hook, made up from an old file, as shown, is used to remove the cotton from the seams. No new cotton should driven in over the old stuff. Further, it is imperative to thoroly clean out all the seams, without leaving trace of hard paint or the old caulking. Then the seams may be brushed clean, with a narrow, stiff wire brush. Be certain that the same amount of cotton is inserted in each seam and do not attempt to tighten up a neighboring seam by driving the plank along the frames

In a large boat, of heavy scantlings, okum is inserted between the planks first and then the cotton is driven in afterwards. The seam is then treated in a similar manner to other caulked seam.

The finished caulking requires the seams to be carefully puttied with white lead putty or other approved seam composition. The seams should be filled even with the surface or with a slight concave by the seam compound pressed tightly into the seams, and the surrounding wood wiped clean of any traces of the compound.

Two or three coats of paint on the exterior of the hull, with sandings between these, will provide a smooth hull and a completely tight one.

After the boat has been in the water for two or three weeks the seams will close up, from the wood absorbing the water, and the seam compound will squeeze flush with the planking and quite possibly protrude further. This condition is a perfectly natural one and must be corrected only by carefully scraping the seams and sanding the topsides. While this swelling and protrusion is likely to occur each year, to a degree, it will be most noticeable in a new boat.

Upon re-reading the above treatise on proper caulking procedures possibly it will be welcome advice ⚓ to both owners and boat yard operators. Particulary to the "would be boat builders" who have set themselves up as proffessionals with little or _no_ experience.

One such builder, whose work we've seen, built a boat recently and a _great_ percentage of the caulking cotton came straight _thru_ the seams. Such a botch job not only creates a particulary poor appearance, but far more important, creates a boat very likely to leak and give trouble in the future. It all comes under the heading of _boat building_ and, of late, we've seen some "GEMS".

With this, your editors will close the Second Book of Boats "Store of Information" and until our next Book will be on the look-out for further information which will make your boating easier, safer and far more enjoyable. ⚓ ⚓

What of the future?

John G. Hanna

THERE was a time when I used to get hundreds of questions every month about every imaginable aspect of boats and boating. The questions still come in, but now all are about just one thing. They run about like this: "How, when, or where can I get some half-way decent boat building lumber at a reasonable price?" And old Mr. Fix-it, who used to tell everybody everything, can only mutter, "I dunno — I only wish I did."

Well, let's haul out the old crystal ball, dust it off, light a stick of incense, mutter a few mystic words, and attempt to gaze into the future.

Ho hum! After staring until my eyes are dim and aching, I regret to report that I can't see anything good. We are just getting over a rather long war, you remember, in which the military men were endowed with an absolutely unlimited blank check. They used a large part of it in an almost successful effort to chop down every tree in the land and convert it into lumber to build training camps, including thousands of entirely unnecessary structures. The supply in this once heavily forested land is running short now. Expert foresters say there is only enough left for 20 years more. After that, if we want any lumber, we will have to import it from the still heavily forested equatorial belts of South America and Africa, and the forests still in the far north of Russia and Siberia. Trees are cheap there, but by the time you add the cost of much handling and a long oversea journey and more handling and milling and storage, 1968 lumber prices will make today's seem like a 5 and 10¢ store.

But hold on, boys. I am not summoning you to a lodge of sorrow. Let's sit down on the edge of the dock and look the situation in the eye frankly. Ever since the world began, or at least ever since man adopted tokens called money as a medium of exchange, prices have been climbing steadily. How many of you know that scarce a hundred years ago, when we were beginning to produce that famous fleet of clipper ships, the standard wage for expert ship carpenters was just one dollar per day? And a day's work meant *work* from shortly after sunrise to sunset — not about three hours of production plus five hours of dawdling around and gossiping like old women.

Look still farther back. Do you remember Mark Twain's famous fantasy, "A YANKEE IN KING ARTHUR'S COURT?" Money was so scarce then that most of the common people never had as much as a penny at a time. So the Yankee introduced that mythical American coin, the mill, a tenth of a cent, for them. Such coins were so tiny he had to invent a tube to carry them, with a trigger to shoot out one at a time. Going still farther back, remember Judas sold Christ for thirty pieces of silver — which wasn't only good for two packs of cigarettes then, but was really a snug little fortune a man could retire on. The farther back in history you go, the cheaper things become in money units. Looking the other way, the more everything will constantly cost, in money units, world without end, forever and ever, amen. It's just one of the inexplicable and unalterable peculiarities of the human ape. Nothing to do but grin and bear it.

Certainly it's no reason to sit down and drag out the old crying towel and do nothing but soak it. Remember your father and grandfather and great-grandfather also had to contend with prices that seemed terribly high to them — and were, balanced against their low wages. Nevertheless they went ahead and built boats regardless. In fact, I'll bet that when, about a million years ago, old John K. Stonehatchet, after hundreds of hours of patient chipping away with his hatchet, and burning with hot rocks, hollowed out a log for the first canoe, most of his tribe said it cost too damn much, and no boat was worth that, and John musta been out in the sun without his hat too long and baked his bean.

So my advice to you is, if you really want a boat—and if you have real cast iron guts like your grandpa's — just mutter "Wottell!" Cinch up your belt, roll up your sleeves, and go ahead and build it, regardless of hell, hurricanes, and high prices. It'll always be worth the cost, as it always was. Sailing over blue water, or gray water and rough, as it often is, is still the most fun us land-crabs can ever get out of life.

Mr. Hanna wrote the above article shortly before his death. It is the last of the written words of John G. Hanna, whom William Washburn Nutting aptly called "The Sage of Dunedin," and we are honored and proud to be able to present it to our readers.

Few are the men who go through life completely in love with their work and few are the men who have produced such excellent and wholesome seagoing yachts as the late John G. Hanna. (1891-1948)   J. A.

Blue Feather's modified skipjack Margretta Lea

I N inflationary times, which like evil seasons come and go, a little
hooker built to Blue Feather's design is an entirely practical and suitable answer to the question of obtaining the *most* boat for the *least*
amount of money. You will not only have the *most* boat in the manner
of accommodations but will also have an exceptionally sea-worthy and
able boat coupled with the ability to sail well.

Remember *Tally Ho!* owned by Mr. Edward N. Wigton? And the
little Chesapeake skipjack plans which were drawn—"To Take the
Place of *Tally Ho!*"—in THE FIRST BOOK OF BOATS? Blue Feather's
boat has a hull form which compares closely to the Atkin designed boat;
'tho the hull form is about the only similar feature of these two boats.
The Messrs. Worth Holden and Harry Hoffman, co-designers of

Margretta Lea, had a client with wholly different ideas about the purposes for which his skipjack would be used, than did our friend of many years "Newt." Wigton. Mr. Wigton, and his daughter Joan, intend to use their skipjack, which we'll refer to as design No. 540 for convenience sake, primarily for day sailing with the small cuddy forward merely as a spot in which to get out of the weather and perhaps change from shore clothes to bathing suit. The Wigtons did not, by any means, expect to use their boat for extended cruises or living aboard. But the *Margretta Lea* has an owner who wants to do *day sailing* as well as to have fairly complete accommodations for two to *cruise* comfortably. And from the appearance of her layout, her designers have aptly fulfilled these requirements. Upon close examination of these plans, and of the plans of design No. 540, shown on pages 86 to 93 of THE FIRST BOOK OF BOATS, there will be a number of major features which make *Margretta Lea* a cruising boat and Mr. Wigton's boat a day sailer. Perhaps it will be interesting to cover a few of these variances. First, and probably foremost, is the entirely water-tight and self bailing cockpit of the *Margretta Lea.* For a self bailing cockpit is the *only* sane type to have in a boat intended for deep water sailing. Altho the wood used in planking, decking and other components would keep her well afloat if swamped, design No. 540 would certainly be a *little* uncomfortable, to say the least, and in a most unsatisfactory position.

Secondly, the *Margretta Lea* is fitted with a trunk cabin, in lieu of the simple raised deck of design No. 540. This moderate trunk cabin provides a much more spacious arrangement with far more headroom. The fore peak will be used for general storage; sails, extra lines, and the hundred-and-one items that manage to get aboard the average small cruising boat. Abaft, to port, there is a 6 ft. 4 in. berth of correct proportions, and, staggered slightly further aft on the starboard side, another large berth is shown.

The galley, to port, is well placed under the companionway hatch. This arrangement will allow fine ventilation and the cook will stand with his head in the hatchway; very comfortable cooking, indeed. Mr. Garden's *Gleam,* shown elsewhere in this book, has the galley amidship and in his schooner the cook sits down at his work. Just another example of the many ways a little boat *may* be arranged to the complete satisfaction of its individual owner. The galley shown in Blue Feather's skipjack is 4 ft. 6 in. long, which is a good sized space for such a little boat. The after end of the trunk cabin, to starboard, shows a large full length hanging locker in which to keep shore clothes in nice order while week-end cruising.

One disadvantage of either *Margretta Lea* or design No. 540, is the large centerboard trunk. This must be contended with, however, and it is possible to use the trunk to advantage by hinging table leaves either side.

No particular type of engine has been specified on the plans, but a 2½ to 5 h.p. moderately slow speed two or four cycle *marine* engine would fit compactly under the bridge deck.

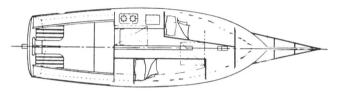

THE SIMPLICITY OF ARRANGEMENT OF THE *Margretta Lea* IS ANOTHER MEANS OF REDUCING COSTS IN OBTAINING A WHOLESOME CRUISING BOAT.

The cockpit is 7 ft. 4 in. long and will allow comfortable sailing for 2 people cruising and up to 4 people while day sailing. Mr. Wigton's boat, on the other hand, will accommodate up to 10 people without over-crowding or approaching an overloaded condition, which again illustrates the reason for a specific design for a specific purpose.

Margretta Lea has 88 sq. ft. of sail area in her staysail and 189 sq. ft. in her main. No. 540 has just 100 sq. ft. more sail area in her two working sails.

The principal dimensions of Messrs. Holden's and Hoffmann's auxiliary are 22 ft. from stem head to top of transom; 18 ft. 9 in. on the designed water line, and 7 ft. 3 in. in breadth. She has a draft of approximately 2 ft. 0 in. with the board up.

We are delighted to be able to show the plans of this interesting little boat to our readers as it is exactly the kind and size of boat we intend to promote in these books—small, wholesome and practical sailing and power craft aboard which may be spent many, many pleasant days under smiling skies and starlit peaceful nights.

Mr. Cleat

A thrash to windward

Oliver Rantanen

I AM the fortunate possessor of one of the finest examples of early
American yachts. Her name is *Nixie;* she was designed by Edward
Burgess and built in 1885 by W. B. Smith and re-built in 1935 by
C. L. Smith, the builder of the Brutal Beast class boats at Marblehead,
Mass. The work on her by these builders was a labor of love, the wood-
work being wonderful.

Nixie measures 23 ft. 7 in. on deck; 20 ft. 6 in. on the water line;
has a breadth of 8 ft.; and a draft of 4 ft. 4 in. The ballast carried is
2000 lbs. of lead outside, and 900 lbs. inside. She carries a gaff main
sail with 330 sq. ft. of canvas; a topsail of 32 sq. ft.; a flying jib of 50
sq. ft.; a jib of 100 sq. ft.; and a staysail of 35 sq. ft. This gives her
about 500 sq. ft. of sail with everything set. Like most of the yachts
of her time she has a plumb bow and a long bowsprit, the latter being
8 ft. in length from the stem head to the cranse iron.

Under full sail *Nixie* is a real little ship. She has never had an
engine to mess her bilge. (However, there have been times when an
engine would have been a comfort — but the thought of this I try to
keep secret.)

The little packet is a marvelous sailing machine and sea-goer. The
summer of 1947 I sailed her to Boothbay, Maine, and back, she performed beautifully. I'll stack her against any modern design of the
same displacement and size. I may be biased but having sailed *Nixie*
under all kinds of conditions I am delighted with her.

About her lines. She was built to sail. There is no propeller or
struts or openings to slow her down so we have a sweet smooth run
from the stem to the after end of the rudder. The result is a boat with
amazing performance in light airs; really ghosts along on a hat-full of
air. In a light breeze she's something to sail and will show a handsome
pair of heels to a surprising number of craft — large and small, old or
new. In a good sailing breeze she's a living, spirited, delightful perfor-
mer. Her deep sharp forefoot holds her well on a close reach to windward in a choppy head sea.

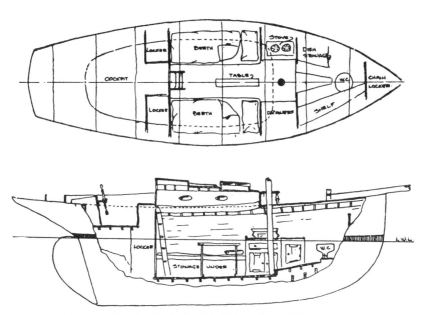

COMPLETE STOWAGE FACILITIES FOR SEA-GOING GEAR ARE INCLUDED IN
Nixie's 23 FT. OF LOVELINESS. ARRANGED FOR THE COMFORTABLE AC-
COMMODATION OF TWO CRUISING COMPANIONS, SHE HAS A CONVEN-
TIONAL, BALANCED LAYOUT, WHICH IS DIFFICULT TO IMPROVE, CONSIST-
ING OF TWO BERTHS, LOCKERS, GALLEY AND "HEAD". A FRESH WATER
TANK IS CONTAINED IN THE CABIN TABLE, AND SPACE FOR "CHOW,
BEER . . . AND OTHER ITEMS DEEMED VITAL".

Coming out of Boothbay heading home we ran into a SW
wind with the tide and the Kennebec River current ebbing. This builds
up the nastiest vertical seas one can visualize. These run about six to
eight feet high, and at the strength of the ebb, off Seguin, when a stiff
SW wind has stirred old man ocean a bit, it's a nasty place. I took
Nixie out and beat into the teeth of it for seven hours. I drove her as
hard as I could to get around Seguin; and around we went, almost to
Cape Small Point. Then the hollow mast split down 6 or 8 ft. (The
hollow mast was the only weak point in her rig. I believe only a solid
stick has any place on a gaff-rigged boat. And that's what went into
her, a new solid stick, and now she's ready for anything.) This thrash
to windward was the acid test of her ability and she came through with
honors—she's all boat, every inch of her.

In 1946 I took her to Maine single handed and there hangs a tale about my passage to the Isles of Shoals from Gloucester. From my log:

July 9th, 1946. Gloucester, Mass. 06:00. Sky overcast, some low scud flipping past. Wind ESE. (Does not look good but the faint-hearted sailor never got anywhere).

07:15 Underway—Wind South.

09:30 Between Londoner and Thatcher's—sea rough.

10:05 Passed Avery Ledge Bellbouy on starboard, wreck of Liberty ship on starboard, looks sad.

10:19 Light on the north end of the sunken breakwater abeam. Departure for the Isles of Shoals.

11:20 Grey world of fog and scud—Heavy following seas and wind. *Nixie* not quite as fast as the rollers—climbing up and down their backs—fun, this kind of sailing.

Now for the story—

If I had used a little more judgement I would have reefed at 11:20. But it was so exhilirating and marvelous, and the seas and wind came up so gradually, that when I realized that it was time to reef it was a bit late. I weighed it, to reef or not to reef. Finally decided not to because the Isles of Shoals' radar tower was visible, now and then, directly ahead which boosted my morale a bit. I was out in the middle of Ipswich Bay running like mad, all my lowers on and that's plenty, wind increasing and seas building bigger and bigger. They were beginning to break across their tops with plenty of hiss. Everything was exciting but not really dangerous, thanks to the long run of the boat's keel and deep forefoot keeping her from broaching or jibing. The seas and wind kept increasing until she was running almost as fast as the seas. *Nixie* then would get on the fore slopes of the seas and rushing down hill at a grade of 30 degrees would speed along exactly like surf-board riders at Hawaii. For five or six minutes at a stretch she was riding the fore slopes. Those were anxious moments because, at the crest, about half of her rudder would come clear of the water, leaving all too little control, and it was nip and tuck for the last half hour. We finally came into Gosport Harbor in a smother of foam. I was dog-tired and glad to be in. Later in the afternoon I took my dog ashore for his daily ".watering", and meeting one of the local lobster fishermen was greeted with; "Saw you coming in, Mister, you sure were moving, yep, you sure were."

As to her accommodations; right in her bow is the chain locker, aft a foot or so, is the 'head'. Coming back from the bow on the star-

160

LONG A FAMILIAR SIGHT IN AND AROUND NEW
ENGLAND'S HARBORS IS THE EARLY AMERICAN
YACHT *Nixie*. UNDER MR. RANTANEN'S LOVING
HANDS THERE IS NO DOUBT THAT *Nixie* WILL CON-
TINUE TO SAIL FOR MANY MORE YEARS.

ANOTHER SUMMER'S PLEASURE IS JUST DOWN THE
'WAYS—NOTICE THE TURNED FIFE RAIL, LOW TRUNK
CABIN WITH FORWARD END ROUNDED IN AN ATTRAC-
TIVE CURVE, THE OVAL PORTS AND PRACTICAL SKYLIGHT.

board side is, first, a long storage shelf extending to the mast. This is a
good place to stow spare sails. Then, the icebox and a set of drawers
for the eating utensils; then the starboard bunk which is also a seat;
then the closet for clothes. In the stern is a large stowage space for all
sorts of gear, spare rope, anchors, etcetera. On the port side, moving
aft; first the dish locker; then the two Primus stoves, and the cabinet
that covers these when out of use; then the port bunk which is also a
seat. And last, the port clothes locker. Under the two bunks is stowage
for chow, beer, gingerale, whiskey or any other item deemed vital to
a successful season afloat. In the middle of the floor it the table which
has a water tank in its inards. The cockpit is large and deep and so
gives plenty of protection in a heavy wind, and is self bailing. She has
a wheel and the housing of the quadrant forms a comfortable seat with
your legs hanging in the cockpit.

Thus is little *Nixie;* an excellent example of yacht design and construction and an exceptionally fast and able craft. Despite her 63
years she is a revelation to all who know her smartness and ability—a
surprise to the owner's of modern yachts from which, on any point of
sailing, she so easily walks away.

162

"Let's see—sail gives way to steam—or is it the other way 'round?"

163

Cruising schooner Gleam

William Garden

THE thirty-foot schooner, *Gleam* hails from Seattle, Washington. The climate there is kind enough to make year-'round sailing possible and Mr. William Garden, her owner-designer, complains good naturedly about this because it is sometimes detrimental to his designing and building business. It's easy to see, though, why he has this trouble — the little hooker *is* trim, and extremely ship-shape.

Several little things, that might first escape attention make her particularly unique. For example, Mr. Garden has a power winch mounted on the starboard side of the small deckhouse over the engine. This winch, hooked up to the engine with a power take-off fitting, makes it possible to raise the anchor without leaving the cockpit; as the anchor chain leads

Gleam UNDER HER THREE LOWERS ON A WINTER'S DAY SAIL.

forward and over a roller chock on the bowsprit. There is a small cylindrical tank provided under the deck for chain storage.

Another thing about *Gleam* that might not be noticed at casual glance is the galley. Mr. Garden doesn't believe in sacrificing the ship-shape qualities of a small cruising boat for the sake of full headroom. He says: "Standing is done on deck." Therefore, *Gleam's* headroom is 4 ft. 10 in. This presented the problem of arranging a handy galley.

164

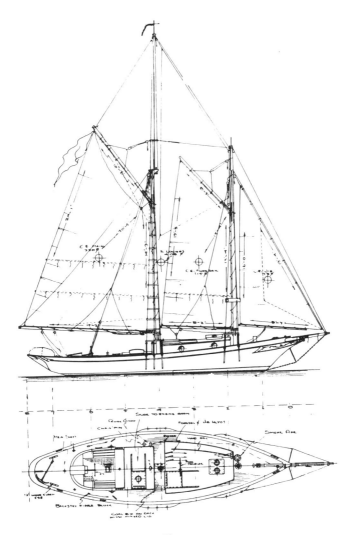

MR. BILL GARDEN'S SCHOONER *Gleam* IS THE RESULT OF HIS OWN ABIL-
ITY AND IS AT PRESENT GIVING HIM YEAR 'ROUND PLEASURE. A CAREFUL
INSPECTION OF THE ABOVE REPRODUCED SAIL AND DECK PLAN INDI-
CATES MR. GARDEN'S STRONG DESIRE FOR SOLID COMFORT AND EASE OF
HANDLING. THE SCHOONER RIG, IN MOST ALL BOATS ATTRACTIVE, IS
WELL CHOSEN FOR THIS LITTLE BOAT.

165

There is a hatch forward but it's not very convenient to cook with your head sticking out of a hatch so the solution was to arrange the galley so one could cook sitting down. Many a housewife might object to such an innovation but any man who has ever worked in the kitchen wonders why in the world his wife feels she must stand up all day over the proverbial hot stove. Whatever the average house-wife's feelings are when she is home, she will *have* to sit down to her culinary chores if she comes aboard *Gleam*. It is a little simpler, of course, to work out such an arrangement in a boat than it is in a house because the galley is small to begin with and everything can be reached handily from a sitting position. The stool, on which one sits while working in the galley, is removable; it serves both the galley and the drop leaf table by simply turning around. An additional practical touch is a miniature chopping block which is flush with the cabin floor and rests on the stem knee.

Mr. Garden happens to like channels and since he feels that there should be a good reason for everything he says that they were installed on both fore and main to give better clearance when walking on the deck. This is certainly true but there is no question but that they do add to the appearance of the boat.

There are a number of drawbridges in the area where *Gleam* does most of her cruising and during some parts of the night these are untended, therefore her owner has a heel rope permanently rove and an oak fid on the bolster so the topmast can be lowered when occasion demands.

For light sails he much prefers the topsail and fisherman's staysail to a Genoa. The former are simpler to work than a Genoa and the high area of the topsail heels her down nicely in a light breeze. In going about, with everything set, all that is involved is setting up the backstays, dipping the fisherman under the spring stay and sheeting it down. Incidentally, there are backstays on the topmast; Mr. Garden neglects to show these on the sail plan. The boat handles easily under three lowers and her topsail and, except downwind in a lumpy sea, the back stays needn't be set up. The jib sheet is dead-ended to starboard and then run through a block on the club boom and aft on the port side. By simply shifting the block fore and aft on the club, the jib may be set flat or full.

The masts are of fir and the booms, spruce. The main topmast is hollow with 5/16ths in. walls, and rigging is 1/4 in. dia. galvanized wire rope set up with deadeyes and Italian hemp lanyards. Decks are 1 1/4 in.

166

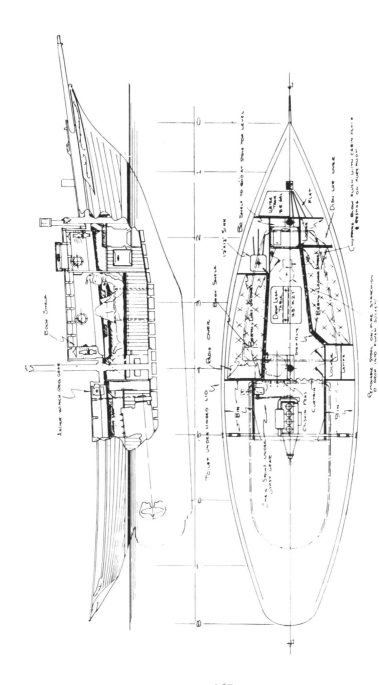

COMBINING SCIENTIFIC, ARTISTIC AND PRACTICAL ABILITIES, MR. GARDEN'S *Gleam* IS A PLEASANT COMBIN-ATION OF THE THREE.

by 1¼ in. fir, caulked and painted. The house trim, coamings and hatches are of teak. Engine house and deckhouse sides are painted white as are the rails. Topsides are black, boot-top white, bottom green. The cabin interior is Alaskan cedar and teak—all varnished.

Gleam is powered with a Palmer engine, model LLH, which develops 20 horsepower at 1400 turns per minute and she cruises at 6 miles per hour with the engine turning 900 R.P.M. There are accommodations for sleeping two in the main cabin. The compact galley has a large locker on the starboard side aft as well as a wood burning cooking stove and sink. There is also excellent storage space under the bunks. In addition there is storage space in the engine compartment which is separated from the main cabin by a curtain.

The schooner is 30 ft. 6 in. over all by 23 ft. 3 in. on the waterline by 8 ft. 6 in. breadth and 3 ft. 10 in. draft.

As we said before, it is little wonder that Mr. Garden plays hookey from work occasionally to cruise in this pleasant little boat.

Mr. Garboard.

A second tribute to the same dinghy

John Atkin

M ABEL is a famous little boat. As RUDDER magazine's *Lark* has become a classic in cat boat design, little *Mabel* has become a classic in small flat-bottom dinghy design. Her plans have been published the world over. They were first shown to the boating public in MOTOR BOAT magazine, affectionately known as "the old green sheet", when Billy Atkin was doing a series of designs for that paper, some twenty-four years ago. Later these appeared in the well-loved magazine FORE AN' AFT with an article in connection with her building by Mr. Weston Farmer. Later *Mabel* showed up in a book published in 1937 entitled MOTOR BOATS written by William Atkin. And recently, while at the National Sportsman's Show, Mr. Al Mason showed me plans of *Mabel* in a current copy of a Norwegian yachting paper he had with him.

It is evident that *Mabel is* a famous little boat.

This little dinghy was designed by William Atkin, in the Mizzentop at Huntington, New York, in October, 1924. She is just as "cocky" and practical today as she was twenty-eight years ago.

There have been many, many sets of blueprints of *Mabel* sold and sent out to all parts of the United States, to the Philippine Islands, England, Germany, Australia, Holland, and to far off India and China. And, during the years past, many letters with photographs enclosed have come back to the office of Atkin & Co. praising the performance of the little boat.

So, it may not be amiss to show the drawings of *Mabel* once again, accompanied by photographs of a very recent edition that was built in the Dinghy Shed behind the office of Anchordown. Mr. Farmer wrote, "You might call *Mabel* a toy if you didn't know her capabilities. You could call her a little work boat or just a son of a gun of a good dinghy, and she would be aptly sufficiently described".

At the gunwale, inside the moulding, the dinghy is 3 ft. 8 in. in breadth. She is 10 ft. 0 in. overall, 9 ft. 0 in. on the waterline; and has a draft of 3½ in. The lines show no ordinary "rowboat". *Mabel's* lines are based on experience and on the performance of many other flat bottomed boats. They show a well-balanced little craft and one that will row well. Her topsides have unusual flare which increases her displacement as a load is put aboard, and also keeps her dry. Her stern is pinched in and the bottom gradually pulled up so that she leaves the water easily. The sheer is graceful. She is, in all, a fine example of a flat-bottomed dink. And for all the arguments against flat-bottomed boats the latter have many factors well worth considering. Such boats can be beached easily in shoal water, they tow well and without difficulty, they are stable and not so dangerously "quick" as some round bilge moulded models I've stepped into, they are easy to pull out on a float, and are much easier to build than a round bilged boat, therefore much less expensive, and, if properly designed, will prove highly satisfactory in every way.

During the past winter Mrs. Edgar L. Stonington, of Darien, Conn., came by to ask me if I would like to build a small rowing boat for her grandchildren's use. She also mentioned that she'd take the little boat rowing herself when the opportunity came. But her main purpose was to have the children learn the fundamentals of rowing, seamanship, and small boat handling, in a first class boat.

After some discussion of various types, proposed uses and costs, Mrs. Stonington decided that *Mabel* would suit her requirements nicely. And so work began.

170

An accurate account of the time spent on the boat is listed below. Each hour was accounted for from the time taken in laying down the lines to the application of the final coat of varnish.

Laying down the lines.	2 hours
Building forms and setting them in proper position.	4 hours
Shaping stem, cutting rabbet and making stem knee.	1½ hours
Gluing up transom, shaping and setting up.	2 hours
Bending and cutting chines, installing these.	5 hours
Preparing template, shaping and fitting bottom strakes, both sides.	3 hours
Preparing template, shaping and fitting two top strakes, both sides.	6 hours
Installing bottom planks, athwartship.	3½ hours

Boat now turned over:

Installing frames, quarter knees and breast hook.	7 hours
Installing seat risers and thwarts.	5 hours
Shaping and fixing half round moulding.	3 hours
Installing sister keelsons.	½ hour
Installing keel and skeg.	2 hours
Sanding hull prior to varnishing.	3 hours
5 coats of spar varnish, application only.	2 hours
3 coats of red copper antifouling compound, application only.	1 hour
2 coats of outside buff on interior bottom.	½ hour
Total —	51½ hours

Cost of materials follow:

Philippine mahogany @ .30 a board foot.	$12.00
White cedar @ .17 a board foot.	3.40
White oak @ .13 a board foot.	3.00
White pine @ .32 a board foot.	2.52
Polished bronze oarlocks and sockets.	2.95
Polished bronze ring bolt.	1.00
Copper cut nails and burrs.	.45
Everdur bronze screws (various sizes).	5.20
Oars, fitted with leathers and copper tips.	6.45
Miscellaneous materials as paint, varnish.	2.60
Total —	$39.81

FIG. 6. *Mabel* NEARING COMPLETION IN THE DINGHY SHED. PHILIPPINE MAHOGANY TOP SIDES, WHITE OAK STEM AND WHITE CEDAR BOTTOM ARE IDEAL BOAT BUILDING WOODS.

It is interesting to note that when Mr. Farmer built *Mabel* in 1927, all the lumber required for the boat cost $15.00, following out the design as to the right wood in the right place, and so on. The most expensive items were the bronze screw fastenings, which cost about $3.00.

I undertook the job of building Mrs. Stonington's boat for $145.00. The accompanying figures show that a total of $39.81 was spent on materials and a total of 51½ hours was spent in building the boat. As I was doing the boat without any particular view for profit, perhaps my time was a little high. In any event the cost of the materials left $105.19 to be divided into a theoretical figure paid for time and profit. If I had paid a top-rate boat builder $1.30 an hour for 51½ hrs. or a total of $66.95, my income, without overhead, would have been $38.24. With overhead and other expenses included, it would boil down to about 25% profit, which is not bad. Enough about costs and figures in general. They are not my favorite pastime.

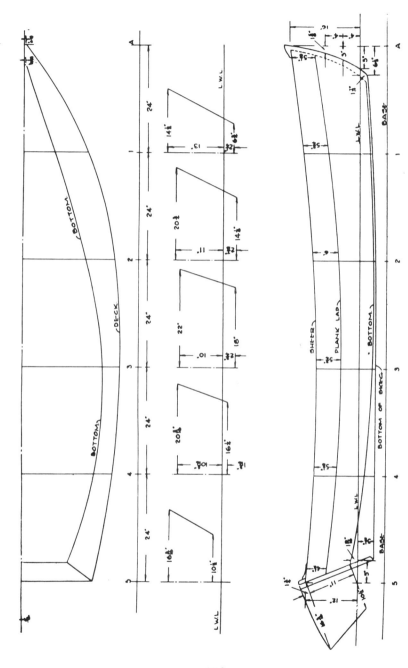

LINES OF THE FLAT BOTTOM SKIFF *Mabel* WITH OFFSETS GIVEN AT EACH STATION.

173

The lines were drawn full size on a sheet of detail paper which was 36 in. wide and about 12 ft. long. This was laid down on the shop floor, with a piece of straight edged 3/4 in. by 6 in. wood nailed to the floor and used as a base line. The perpendicular station lines were drawn at the distances indicated on the line drawings. Then the water-line was snapped in place using a chalked line.

First the sheer line was drawn with a long batten of white pine about 3/4 in. sq. in the middle and gradually tapering at each end. The bottom sweep was next and then the deck and bottom of the plan view were drawn atop the profile. On such a simple boat as *Mabel* the lines are an easy proposition to lay down. On a larger boat, with many waterlines, diagonals, and buttocks, the process of laying down requires a great deal of time—time well spent however. And the only correct way to start building *any* kind of boat.

The sections were drawn in next, the distances taken from the full size drawing, and *not* from the blueprint. The fore and aft lines should always be laid down and faired up first. The body plan is then drawn from these. This will tend to correct any small inaccuracies which may appear in the original scale drawings. When we finished the work, the stem, with its rabbet, back rabbet and bearding line were all laid down on the detail paper, along with the bevels of the frames and the transom.

I believe that laying down the lines is one of the most interesting and thought-provoking tasks entailed in boat building. It is certainly the most important and should be done with the greatest care. The successful outcome of the finished boat results in the care, time and accuracy taken in laying down the boat in the very beginning.

I cut the stem from a piece of 2 in. sided white oak—free from knots or poor grain. A piece of 1/8 in. Tekwood was slipped under the detail paper and the outline of the stem, with the rabbets, sheer line and bottom pricked through. This was cut out, as a template, and then trans-ferred to the oak. When the stem was completed I gave it two coats of linseed oil and turpentine, (mixed one part oil to four parts turps.) This penetrated the oak and prevented checking.

The forms were made next. These were of 3/4 in. eastern pine and were carefully screw-fastened and braced to the floor to take the strain of the chine pieces and the planking, when the time came for bending and fastening these. All the dimensions were taken from the "mould loft" floor—from the sections drawn full size. A batten was fastened

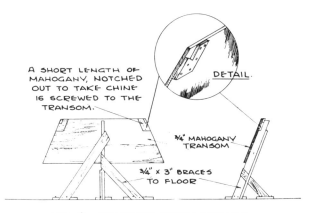

A SHORT LENGTH OF
MAHOGANY, NOTCHED
OUT TO TAKE CHINE
IS SCREWED TO THE
TRANSOM.

DETAIL.

¾" MAHOGANY
TRANSOM

¾" X 3" BRACES
TO FLOOR

FIG. 2. SHOWING STERN DETAILS.

to each of the forms and to the stem knee to keep these properly spaced until the chines were fitted.

Each of the forms was spaced 24 in. apart according to the line drawing. Setting up the stem and stern at the correct angles was rather difficult. There was not a great deal to fasten these to somehow, and I found myself looking for a "sky hook" or other suitable device to hold the transom and stem in place. With various braces, lots of measuring and a tremendous amount of genuine cussing, they were eventually located satisfactorily and securely fastened.

White oak, ¾ in. by 1½ in., was used for the chines. Oak has many great advantages, among which are its fastening-holding power, ability to bend, non-splitting qualities, and straight, clear grain. I did not have a steam box and did not feel much like making one at the moment. Consequently the chines were bent cold, first being clamped to the stem, and then on each form, working aft to the stern. A Chinese windlass, or tourniquet, was used at the stern to get the two chines secured to the transom. This was not very satisfactory in many ways. The end grain of the transom would not hold the screw fastenings because of the tension the oak exerted. It was not possible to get more than two fastenings in the end of the chine, as the dimensions limited it to only two. After several unsuccessful attempts at fastening the chines to the transom, I unclamped these and tapered the after ends to ½ in. in a length of 24 in. I also screwed a short length of mahogany to the transom, notched out to take the chine, and to act as a stern frame. As illustration 2 shows, this was placed with the grain running verti-

175

cally. The chines were then put back in place and pulled in much more easily. The screws were driven into the new partial stern frame and held successfully.

Next time I build a skiff I shall set up a stern frame and let the chines run past this. Later I'll cut the chines off flush with the frame and put the transom in place. It will make the work much easier and will eliminate the difficult job of measuring the chines to fit "inside" the transom, along with the complicated double bevel. A steam box would have made things much easier and the time taken building one would have been well spent. But, like many things, it seemed like quite an undertaking for the little time it would be in use.

With the forms set up, the stem and transom in place and the chines in, little *Mabel* began to look like a boat. I called Mrs. Stonington and asked her to come and "inspect" the boat. She did and was not, I'm afraid, very much impressed.

I was very fortunate in having some well-seasoned Philippine mahogany of pre-war quality. This was in 10, 12 and 14 foot lengths and in thicknesses of $\frac{3}{8}$, $\frac{1}{2}$ and $\frac{7}{8}$ in. Officer Hugh McManus, one of Darien's finest, purchased the mahogany before the war with the intention of building *Betty Carroll,* a 28 ft. power boat. The war came dis-

FIG. 3. TWO LOWER STRAKES IN PLACE. FORMS AT STATIONS NO. 1 AND 2 CAN BE SEEN.

rupting his plans. Upon his return he undertook a smaller boat, and not needing all his mahogany, let me have the surplus.

I used ¼ in. yellow pine for a template of the bottom strake and clamped this in place marking around the chine, stem and stern to obtain the outline. To get the proper curve for the top edge of the plank, a batten was tacked on the forms, and this curve was transferred to the template.

The two bottom strakes, each side, were then roughed out, finished off smoothly and put in place. The same procedure was used for the next strakes. Fig. 3 shows the stem of the dinghy, with the two lower strakes in place. I cut a rabbet in the strake edges at the stem and stern, so that they ended up flush each end. This rabbet can be seen in the top edge of the strake in the photograph. Starting back about 18 in. from the end of the plank, with the full thickness of the plank, a

FIG. 4. A METH-
OD OF OBTAINING
A FLUSH SEAM AT
STEM OR STERN.

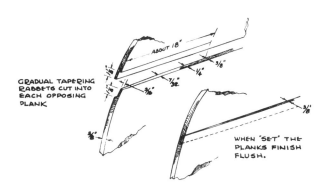

GRADUAL TAPERING RABBETS CUT INTO EACH OPPOSING PLANK

WHEN "SET" THE PLANKS FINISH FLUSH.

gradual, tapered rabbet was cut into the edge of the plank. A similar rabbet, on the reverse side, was cut in the opposing plank. When the two were set up they were actually halved and came together flush at the ends. Fig. 4 shows the method used, probably more clearly than my writing.

The strakes were fastened at both the stem and stern with ⅞ in. number 8 Everdur bronze screws. They were temporarily held in place on the forms with iron screws, having wooden washers under the heads to prevent scarring the surface of the mahogany. There was no difficulty getting the strakes bent around, despite the fact that there is quite a strong twist at the after ends of the bottom ones.

The bottom of the dinghy was planked athwartship with ⅝ in. by 4 in. white cedar, starting at the bow and proceeding toward the stern. The narrow widths of the planks will eliminate buckling and therefore assure water-tightness. I hauled *Mabel* out of the water recently, and her bottom was as smooth as the day it was launched—with no sign of buckled or checked planks. A slight V cut was made in the chine edge to take a single strand of cotton wicking. This was laid down in fresh paint, and the plank then fastened down, squeezing the cotton tightly between it and the chine.

The bottom was Everdur bronze screw-fastened. While such fastenings take a while longer to drive and are more expensive than nails, I believe they are well worth the extra time and cost—even in a small flat-bottomed dinghy such as *Mabel*.

When the bottom and topsides were planed and sand-papered the owner was again called for "inspection". This time she was much more pleased, but was "amazed" to see the boat had a flat bottom.

I had the devil's own time locating cut copper nails. Visiting hardware stores became a sorry task. Clerks told me all kinds of tales, some amazingly stupid, some downright lies. One told me that cut nails hadn't been manufactured since the days of horses and carriages. Knowing of my search for copper cut nails, my life long friend, Mr. M. Bruce Conklin, turned up one day with a pound of the cut nails with burrs to suit. These were about 1¼ in. long and about 3/32 in. up under the head tapering to 1/32 in. at the points; purchased from a store at Bridgeport, Conn.

Being so tapered, the burr, or copper washer, drives up snugly, and very tightly. Such cut nails are far superior to the common copper nail, which is round and parallel sided. These rivets were spaced about 2½ in. apart and staggered on the plank edges. The planks lapped over approximately 1 in.

After twenty or more rivets were set up along each lap in the strakes, the boat was removed from the forms and turned over, and made ready for the fitting of the side frames. These were made of ⅞ in. white oak, 2 in. at the bottom of the boat, tapering to 1 in. at the gunwale. A template, of ¼ in. yellow pine, was made for each frame. As shown in the photograph of the interior of the boat, Fig. 5, the frames are notched out and fit snugly against the planking.

A visit to a neighboring deserted apple orchard provided the quarter knees and a natural crook from an old cherry tree eventually

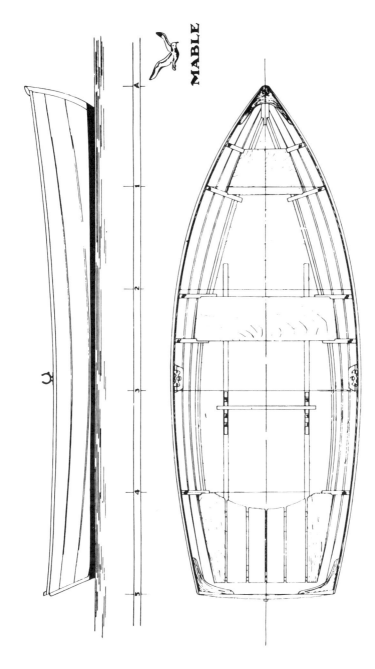

MABLE

"WE SHOULD HAVE MORE *Mabels*. SIMPLE, PRIM LITTLE BOATS . . ." OUTBOARD PROFILE AND INTERIOR ARRANGEMENT ARE REPRODUCED ABOVE. ROWING FOOT STOP IS ADJUSTABLE TO SUIT PERSON ROWING.

179

FIG. 5. INTERIOR OF *Mabel* LOOKING FORWARD.

became the breast hook. All of these were used green and it's interesting to note that the apple, as it dried, did not change shape, check, or change form in any manner. The cherry breasthook did develop a slight check, but nothing very serious. These were coated with a mixture of linseed oil and turpentine immediately after they were shaped.

After the frames, breast hook, quarter knees and sister keelsons were in place the boat was turned over again to have the skeg and keel fitted and put in place.

Philippine mahogany ¾ in. by 4 in. was used for the keel. This was screw-fastened to each of the bottom planks with 1½ in. Everdur bronze screws.

The after end of the keel had two parallel saw cuts taken in it the length and thickness of the skeg, the piece between not being cut out. The skeg was then slipped up under the strip formed by the saw cuts and fastened securely to the bottom planks and to the stern post. This method allows the keel to run full length and does away with any joints at the forward end of the skeg, joints that always pick up seagrass, sand, and the like.

A half-round oak moulding was screwed along each side at the gunwale. The moulding was allowed to protrude above the sheer plank and was later planked down flush, making a flat surface at the sheer, which looks very well.

Oak seat risers, ¾ in. by 1½ in. were screwed to the frames. The seats were of white pine ¾ in. by 12 in. wide. These were left an inch away from the sides of the boat so that sand and muck would not get under them when the boat was turned up on its side to empty. The stern sheets were slatted and these were of ½ in. white pine, the slats extending fore and aft.

180

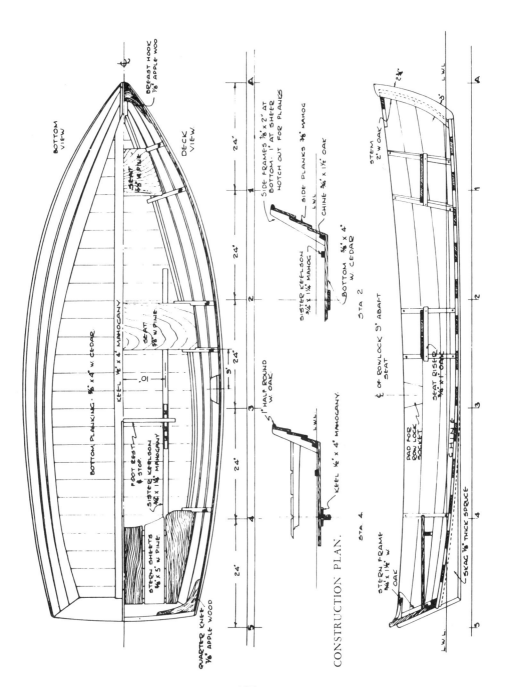

CONSTRUCTION PLAN.

FIG. 7. *Mabel* COMPLETED. THIS LITTLE BOAT WAS CHRISTENED *Precious*
BY MRS. STONINGTON'S GRANDCHILDREN.

Sanding and varnishing the hull is very satisfying work. The results of your labor have really taken form and the prospect of seeing the little boat finished and afloat is very close.

I applied two coats of spar varnish to the top sides before any putty was used. If putty or oil of any kind is put on the bare wood it will make a stain which is impossible to remove. No wood fillers were used in the finish.

A single coat of white lead paint was applied to the bottom and it was then puttied. The bottom planks were fitted closely with a slight outgauge on each but no caulking cotton was used.

Five coats of varnish were applied, the wood being carefully sanded and wiped off between each coat. The finish looked very handsome when the boat left the shop and later, at the time she was ready for winter stowage, still had a nice gloss and lustre.

Three coats of Interlux red copper anti-fouling compound were put on the bottom.

The little skiff weighed exactly 100 lbs. complete, according to the Fairbanks scale at the local lumber yard.

She did take in a little water through the bottom for about 12 hours, then tightened up and stayed tight all summer, except in one spot where two holes were drilled and only one rivet was driven through—here a tiny "squirt" of water came aboard whenever weight was put on its side.

When launched and tried *Mabel* proved again, as did her predecessors, that she was dry, rowed easily and straight, with no fuss, carried three people comfortably and was ideal for two.

The accompanying photographs, Figs. No. 6, 7, and 8, show *Mabel* while still under construction in the Dinghy Shed, a view of the interior just outside the door and another where she is water-borne, resting lightly on the water.

Mabel was built as closely to the plans as possible. And as Mr. Farmer wrote, "We should have more *Mabels*. Simple, prim, little boats—a joy to own, to build, to pay for. You can't ask much more from any boat, particularly when you get good looks, easy rowing, good disposition, and husky lightness t'boot".

FIG. 8. *Precious,* NEE *Mabel,* WATERBORNE DURING HER BUILDER'S TRIALS.

183

Mr. Charles G. Davis, prolific writer of the sea and expert model maker. On a recent visit we found him busy and happy in the process of completing an exquisite model of the half-brig *John A. McDermott* for Mr. John A. McDermott of Midland, Texas.

GAUNTLET'S STORMY TRIP TO BERMUDA by C·G·DAVIS

M OST yachting stories begin at daybreak, but this one is just the opposite. Many people were thinking of retiring when the little
sloop *Gauntlet* weighed anchor off Bayonne, N. J., and drifted
silently along through the Staaten Island Kills, as the old Dutch settlers
named that narrow body of water which pours out of Newark Bay
around Bergen Point toward New York Bay.

On the water all was still, save for an occasional tug passing up
against the tide or the hurried rush of the ferry boat like an immense
glow worm throwing the reflection from its cabin lights far up and
down the river as it splashed from shore to shore. *Gauntlet,* painted
black as night herself, with one red and one green light twinkling across
the water and her white sails reflecting an occasional light from the
Staaten Island shore, drifted on toward the Bay.

Sailing the *Gauntlet* was her owner, George W. Robinson, a tall,
slenderly built young fellow. Near him, keeping look-out for approaching boats and helping him sail the sloop, sat his mate, a young bride,
who was spending her honeymoon with him in this novel manner.

By the time the sloop had drifted into the Bay, a fresh breeze
picked up and the little boat heeled well over, made the white water

roar under her stubby bows as she drove along through the Narrows and on into Gravesend Bay where, at midnight, she came to anchor.

To promote amateur seamanship in small boats, Sir Thomas Lipton had offered a thousand-dollar cup to the winner of a race from Gravesend Bay, New York Harbor to St. David's Head Bermuda. The race was started by the officials of the Brooklyn Yacht Club, and timed at the finish by officials of the Royal Bermuda Yacht Club. Boats were limited in over all length to forty feet and no professional sailors were allowed to be on board.

It was in anticipation of this race that Mr. and Mrs. Robinson had bought the *Gauntlet* and made all preparations for an ocean trip.

When, therefore, no judges had come on board up to the morning of the race, May 26, 1906, although the *Gauntlet* had been at anchor twenty-four hours before the starting time, (as required by the rules governing the races, in order to give the judges time to inspect each boat and pass their judgement as to whether she was eligible to race or not) the skipper began to fear that all their well laid and long contemplated plans might meet with a hitch.

So, leaving his mate to continue stowing away the stores, he rowed ashore to make inquiries. The judges informed him the *Gauntlet* would not be allowed to start as a competitor with a woman aboard the boat.

He called their attention to a printed circular giving the conditions governing the race and there was nothing in the circular to prohibit it.

But the committee seemed to feel the responsibility of sending a yacht off to sea on a race with a woman aboard more than they cared to shoulder.

When Mr. Robinson told them the *Gauntlet* was going to Bermuda whether as a competitor or not, and that the same woman they were kicking about could handle a boat as well as most men, they adjourned and promised to send an early answer out to the yacht.

The water tank was refilled and fifteen extra one-gallon stone jugs were stowed aft under the cockpit in oakum to prevent breaking. Ice, provisions, a surpise in the shape of half a crate of fresh eggs, and a dozen broilers from friends on a chicken farm, completed their stores.

At one o'clock the committee had sent no word, but preparations went steadily on aboard the *Gauntlet*. The spinnaker pole and club topsail were lashed fast on deck, plugs for the cockpit scuppers were whittled out and the steering gear was well greased. Useless fittings such as boom crotch, sail covers, camp chairs, and several empty dress suit cases were taken ashore.

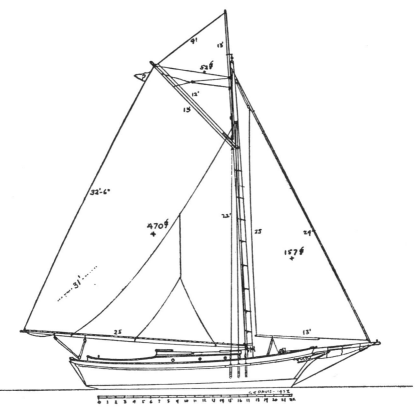

SAIL PLAN OF **GAUNTLET.**

Two o'clock found the Skipper putting the finishing touches on the overhauling of the *Gauntlet's* jib sheets, which he had changed to suit a new jib with its foot cut high to prevent its filling with water, as the old one would do, at times, from the wash of the lee bow wave.

Below, his mate tried to hold back great tears of mortification. Months of anticipation and dreaming of this ocean trip were to be realized or shattered at one word by the chairman of the race committee and so it was with a quickening pulse they watched the approach of the committee boat at quarter past two.

The verdict was favorable. While the judges didn't like the idea of sending a woman off on an ocean trip that many men would be afraid

187

to take, there were no real grounds for prohibiting her participating in the race and the skippers of the two yawls had both threatened to withdraw if *Gauntlet* was barred. Sailing instructions were passed to the *Gauntlet's* crew and the racing letter U, pinned to her mainsail, while two committeemen examined the life buoys, etc., to see that all were up to the requirements.

At half past two the balance of *Gauntlet's* crew, Mr. J. S. Dunlap, the navigator, and Mr. Henry Higgins, who volunteered to cook, had not yet arrived, although the other competitors, the yawls *Tamerlane* and *Lila,* with all hands aboard ready for the gun were sailing about. *Gauntlet* wished them good luck as they passed. Both yawls were larger boats, carrying six men, and had to allow the *Gauntlet* considerable time, she being very much smaller, with only half the sail spread. The sympathy of most of the spectators was with the little black sloop and her unusual crew. A substantial token of this sympathy, in the form of a rabbit's foot and a box of candy, was passed aboard from a party of friends in a launch, who wished them good luck just as the navigator and cook came aboard.

Five minutes before the preparatory gun, sail was hoisted on *Gauntlet,* the anchor hove up and securely lashed, and with a stiff southerly wind that came in across the bay from "old ocean", she stood for the starting line about which the two yawls were maneuvering.

Gauntlet, standing for the line, crossed two seconds too soon, and was recalled, letting the two larger yawls take the lead. She wheeled around and recrossed the line again, losing some little time by the maneuver.

When a southerly breeze pipes up off Sandy Hook and seas roll in over the shoals in the Lower Bay, they cause considerable activity aboard small yachts, which jump and splash and foam along just as the bluff-ended little *Gauntlet* was now doing.

Ahead of her, standing down the ship channel and jumping hard into the head seas, went the two yawls, almost indistinguishable amid the accompanying fleet of spectators, drawing away from the sloop.

As it was a thrash dead to windward either way to gain the open sea, the *Gauntlet's* crew put her about and stood out Ambrose Channel as the quickest way of getting off the shoals into the longer, easier, deep water swells that would not toss their craft about so recklessly.

By doing this, she separated from her rivals and stood on out to sea, accompanied for a time by the handsome schooner yacht *Swab,* passing abeam of the Sandy Hook lightship at six o'clock, and keeping

company with the big steam pilot boat that ran alongside of her to leeward for several miles, the latter giving them a cheer and several salutes
of the weird sounding siren whistle as she left them, in token of good-
by and good luck.

Little did the crew of *Gauntlet* know what was happening to
their rivals out of sight near Sandy Hook. Larger and more powerful
boats, both of them, they were thrashing ahead smashing down the seas
and getting to windward faster than *Gauntlet,* but the pace told on the
Lila. Her main mast suddenly broke at the jaws of her gaff and down
came all her gear, a mass of tangled wreckage. Whether *Tamerlaine* put
back out of sympathy for *Lila* in her misfortune or whether her crew
dreaded the threatening look in the southern sky, may never be known.
She bore up and ran back to her anchorage with *Lila* in tow of a tug.

Gauntlet's crew knew nothing of all this; night was coming on
black and Bermuda was 650 miles to windward. The sea was getting up
every hour and the wind steadily increasing. *Gauntlet,* while built like a
coasting schooner and having iron enough on her keel to enable her to
carry full sail in a cyclone, heeled over considerably, owing to a very
easy bilge.

Past experience had taught that everything must be secured. The
spars were lashed fast to the oak hand rails that ran along each side of
the cabin top, the halliards in coils were hitched up to the belaying pins.

One feels the solitude of old ocean more in a little craft than on a
large steamer, where the companionship of many passengers lessens the
loneliness; the land, too, disappears from view much more quickly on
the small craft.

And this day, windy, hazy, and raw, even the Highlands of the
Navesink were lost to view, but at 7:30 someone sighted an incoming
steamship about four miles off. One minute she was in sight, the next
she'd settle down behind an ocean surge, till nothing but a funnel and
her spars were in sight, then the little *Gauntlet* would go down the back
of a gray sea and nothing but the next curling wave crest, its edge
fringed with spray, and the sky above, could be seen.

Darkness shut the steamer from view and watches were set on the
sloop. Messrs. Dunlap and Higgins, as navigator and cook in the port
watch, went below where the cheerful light of the cabin lamp gave a
homelike look to the little cabin, and stretched out in questionable comfort, while on deck the owner and his mate, shipped for life's voyage as
well as the present Bermuda trip, kept the little sloop to her course by a
compass seen through a glass set in the forward staving of the cockpit

and lighted by a lamp in the cabin. It blew harder than ever after sunset and the *Gauntlet* swept along under full sail with her lee decks buried under water up to the cabin house.

With heavy underclothing, heavy suits, sweaters and oilskins buttoned up tight, the night wind cut cold and raw into the watch on deck, who turned their caps down over their ears and put on woolen gloves.

The most welcome sight that met the skipper's eyes next morning, Sunday, was a thin curl of blue smoke that came out of the galley pipe and whisked away like a puff from a cigar. From below came sounds suspiciously like an attempt on the cook's part to surprise the hungry, tired watch, but when the odor of frying chicken wafted aft to the skipper at the wheel, a wild whoop of welcome greeted the attempt.

Think of it, hot chicken after a night, wet and cold, and bounced about like dice in a box. When the meal of hot cocoa, chicken and bread, was over there was a feeling of complete satisfaction.

With daylight, the air lost its chill, still the day was heavy and overcast, and the breeze kept hardening gradually with the sea increasing. All day long *Gauntlet* sailed on, east-south-east, with the wind south, but the leeway brought the true course they were making about due east.

Watch in and watch out the *Gauntlet* kept driving along under full sail on her course and by noon had covered 155 miles to windward against wind and sea, an average of over six knots.

All went well until two o'clock Monday morning, when the navigator, becoming somewhat worried by the threatening look in the southern sky, called the "old man" out to take a look. There was trouble coming, and coming fast. Rain, in torrents, was cutting down so hard that it made the flesh smart and blinding flashes of bluish white momentarily blinded the eyes, while ear-splitting claps of thunder rent the air.

Keeping off a point the crew anxiously watched to see if it was a sudden thunderstorm that would pass over as quickly as it had come, but as minutes passed the wind steadily hardened. Mr. Robinson decided to shorten sail before it became too dangerous to go up forward.

"East, east by north, east-north-east", called the mate as fast as she could, while the owner and navigator made preparations to take in the mainsail; the navigator at the wheel, while the skipper, after watching his chance, ran forward and let go the halliards. But, as usual in such circumstances, the throat of the sail stuck and the owner had to drag it down. Despite this the sail was lowered and stopped.

The jib was left set, and somewhat to their surprise the crew found that the sloop traveled along comfortably and looked up well to the wind. So, under this sail alone she traveled until daybreak, when a close reefed mainsail was set. Under this canvas she heeled over to her cockpit coaming, lee rigging and decks dragging through the water, a mass of white foam.

"WHEN A WAVE BROKE AT THE STERN".

By noon the seas were more than it was safe to negotiate and, to prevent getting swamped by the white crested coamers that rolled completely over her, the sloop was squared away before the wind and sea, and the peak of the mainsail lowered. In spite of their best efforts to keep her running true before wind and sea there were times when a sea would toss her about so the sail would jibe over, all standing.

Down in the hollow, the following sea seemed to rush after them, a towering wall of angry water sometimes as much as seventeen feet high.

Up, up this seemingly insurmountable steep sea the sloop would rise, smothered completely in the coaming crest, and carried along for yards at breakneck speed, and attaining an impetus that carried her boiling along buried in spray on the back of the wave.

Then settling down she seemed to be going down into a hole, while all around, the dark seas rose high above them, narrowing their horizon to a very small circle.

Gauntlet was certainly in for a hard time. Excepting the owner every one went below and shut the cabin up tight, leaving him alone at the wheel, to keep her going on her mad race. Time and time again when she had her stern to the sky and her bows pointing for the bottom, the skipper had his heart in his throat for fear she would pitch end over end. And when an extra big wave broke right at her stern and rolled completely over the boat, filling the cockpit flush to the rails, he began to think it was time to heave to.

Passing the end of one of the boom guys about his waist, Mr. Robinson held on until three or four more seas pooped the little craft and nearly knocked him from the wheel. Then he called for the navigator to come on deck and get the dinghy ready as a sea anchor.

While the navigator was putting a heavy lashing around the dinghy and lashing a small anchor to it to sink it so it would hold in the right position, the mate and cook below were preparing a canvas bag. Stuffing it with oakum, soaked with wave oil, they sewed it up for an oil bag. A two hundred-fifty foot 3 in. hawser was made fast to the sea-anchor and made ready to use.

The mate came on deck, and the cabin doors were closely battened down in anticipation of a deluge. Lashed to the wheel she awaited the signal to luff the sloop. The skipper went forward to take in the jib and the navigator stood ready on top of the cabin house to stow the mainsail.

Watching until a lull appeared, the signal to luff was given and all halliards were let go by the run. The sloop rounded up promptly and the sails came down, but before the stops could be put around them, trouble in the shape of an extra large breaker appeared. Robinson on the bowsprit, with his arms about the folds of the jib, went out of sight completely. Dunlap, stowing the mainsail on top of the cabin, was up to his knees in solid water, and Mrs. Robinson at the wheel, catching the full force of the sea, was nearly carried over the side. She clung with strength to the wheel and was still in the boat when the sea, after sweeping *Gauntlet* bodily sideways several yards, passed over and three half drowned people drew a deep breath and more than likely muttered a fervent "Thank God" when they found all were safe.

When the skipper went forward he had on no oilers because the work to be done required perfect freedom. As he lay flat on his stomach to stow the jib he saw the wave coming and clasped the bowsprit to prevent himself from being swept overboard. One pant leg caught on the low chock and ripped the shank covering nearly to the knee as he hastily scrambled inboard. "Where's Dunlap?" was the skipper's first remark as he looked aft and saw no one on deck but his wife. But the navigator was safe, though out of sight behind the folds of the mainsail.

Soaked clothes were of little consequence now; no one had time in the excitement to notice how drenched they all were. With superhuman effort the sails were lashed fast and the skipper and navigator hurried to get the sea anchor over the side.

The drag, contrary to their expectations, failed to head them up toward the sea. Instead, the *Gauntlet* lay broadside on in the troughs and was completely swept by each crest as it broke. Holes were punched in the oil bag and this was put over at the shrouds. The result was marvelous. It did not abate the size of the sea one bit, nothing could stop the fury of the elements then raging, but all the small broken surface was stilled by the oil slick.

Finding that the sloop made fair weather of all the fury she was exposed to, her half drowned crew went below and left her to fight it out alone. Nothing more could be done by men; it was now a test of endurance between the little sloop and the elements, and thankful indeed was her crew that she was the heaviest built sloop of her size in the States.

LITTLE *Gauntlet* HOVE TO IN "OLD OCEAN".

A little square hatch in the cabin top was fitted tight and clamped down with a bar and a set screw, yet every sea that pounded down on her sent water squirting and dripping through on to the already wet crew.

The swinging cabin lamps were useless, none would stay lighted during such wild tossing, and the globes were smashed to fragments. Fortunately they had a supply of cold, cooked meats, canned stuff, pilot bread, crackers, cake and a liberal supply of chocolate, and they fared on this during the bad weather. Higgins, the cook, kept up the cheerfulness of the party by an inexhaustible supply of stories and songs, and when not doing this he was whacking his head on the companionway or getting pitched out of his bunk to land across the cabin, as usual, on his head.

From eight o'clock that night, Monday, until midnight the navigator, encased in oilers to keep warm, not dry, because was out of the question, sat in the cockpit keeping a lonely lookout. He figured they were hove to within about twenty miles of the trans-Atlantic steamship track and also in the path of steamers from Canada to the West Indies.

Soaked to the skin with water at times waist deep as the seas rushed over the *Gauntlet,* he clung fast watching the huge black seas sweep down on the sloop and marveling that she could ever rise to surmount them.

This was certainly yachting with a vengeance. It was life or death, depending on the staunchness of the little 28 foot sloop which was being made a football of by "old ocean". What he would have done had a ship suddenly loomed up is doubtful. They had tried to light the flare-up torch early in the evening, but it blew out as soon as exposed and no lamp would stay lighted in such a wind.

Then their horizon was so limited that they could not see a ship until she was so close that she'd crash into them before they would have time to do anything.

It was one of those times when a sailor simply has to wait and trust that the —

"Sweet little cherub that sits up aloft
keeps watch for the life of poor Jack."

When daybreak came on Tuesday morning the four bedraggled crewmen aboard *Gauntlet* could scarcely believe it real when they looked out to find a beautiful clear sky and a sea, which, while still very heavy, gave signs of moderating.

The cook infused new life into the party by starting a fire in the little stove, and cooking breakfast.

He could, by some magic of his own, have a hot coke fire going in a few minutes, and the aroma of boiling cocoa and warm soup paved the way for a quick consumption of those delicacies when handed 'round in cups.

The generous heat radiating from the stove soon made the cabin

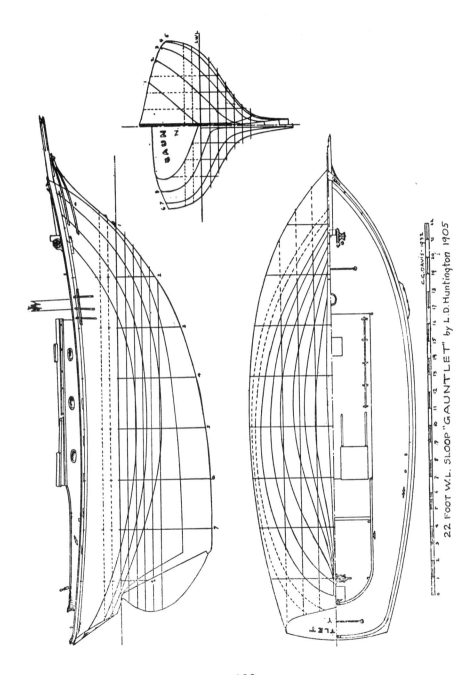

22 FOOT W.L. SLOOP "GAUNTLET" by L.D. Huntington 1905

C.G.DAVIS 1933

warm and comfortable and the *Gauntlet's* crew decided that they better make sail.

The sea anchor was hauled aboard with considerable difficulty and stowed again on deck, the mainsail close reefed and a small jib set.

At noon the navigator got a good observation and their position figured out on the chart put *Gauntlet* 550 miles from Bermuda and 150 miles from New York, Bermuda bearing them south by west, dead to windward. Their rivals, they calculated, were about 100 miles south west of them, figuring that they had held the starboard tack as *Gauntlet* had done. As a matter of fact *Tamerlane* had lain at anchor at the club house in Gravesend Bay all through this southerly storm which drove *Gauntlet* so far to the eastward and had left her anchorage only that same morning, twenty minutes of nine, going off with a stiff northwest breeze before the wind.

All day Tuesday *Gauntlet* bucked into the heavy seas with a succession of squalls that increased in force after sunset, until at one o'clock on Wednesday all hands were again required to take in the mainsail.

The mate, as usual, took the wheel, and when the sail was furled all three men went below and lay down for a rest while she kept the *Gauntlet* sailing along under jib only. Utterly exhausted, the men fell sound asleep, and while they snored away in blissful unconsciousness one little woman sat alone at the wheel for five hours, with nothing but flying spray, waves and hurrying, shadowy clouds overhead to keep her company.

At six o'clock the first sleepy head appeared in the companionway and was justly greeted with, "Well, I thought you men were never going to awaken!"

The rest were routed out and as the wind moderated with the appearance of the sun a single reefed mainsail was set.

As the day advanced the wind moderated still more, so the reef was shaken out and under full sail again *Gauntlet* was pushed to windward.

Once that night the mainsail had to be lowered to avoid one of those vicious white squalls that seem to sweep out of nowhere and hit a vessel with no warning at all.

After that the wind and sea moderated. About 2 a. m. the loneliness of his watch wore on the navigator to such an extent he felt nothing but a pot of cocoa could console him, so stopping the wheel fast he stole quietly into the cabin to make a fire and brewed an excellent pot of cocoa.

When all hands awoke at daylight the reef was shaken out and with sheets lifted by a fair wind, the first of its kind they had had so far, *Gauntlet* was footing fast for Bermuda.

Guesses were made as to their position. At noon, when the navigator got his position figured out, he announced that they were three hundred miles from their goal.

The wind headed them at sunset, so for the first time in five days *Gauntlet* was put about onto the port tack and everything below arranged for the starboard tack had to be shifted to prevent going pell mell into confusion again.

Moving about seemed awkward, so accustomed had they been to the other tack.

At one o'clock Friday morning, as the captain and mate were on watch, the sky in the southwest grew darker and darker with indications of a heavy squall from that quarter. Getting rather nervous about it the navigator was called out to have a look.

He pronounced it nothing at all to worry about and went below to finish out his sleep.

Nothing came of it and at daybreak it had cleared up, so full mainsail was set and *Gauntlet* put about on the starboard tack, the wind having hauled so she could just about lay her course.

As the sun rose higher, the breeze veered more to the west until she was looking up above her course and the balloon jib and club topsail were set. Under this cloud of sail, the little sloop boiled along over the long, easy ocean swells in grand style, rapidly cutting down the distance to Bermuda. New life was infused into all hands, the cook's rising spirits brought additional song and, what was more substantial, he prepared a grand feast.

The mate, now that it was possible to stand safely on deck, got busy with the clothes and cushions, putting them out to dry, until the sloop looked like a clothes line on wash day.

That noon the observation put the yacht 170 miles from Bermuda. The breeze hardened toward sunset, but hauled more ahead, so light sails had to be taken in and the yacht close hauled. That night they were treated to a most beautiful sunset that betokened light winds. In fact, it fell a flat calm for half that night. Nearly all day two beautiful white gulls flew around the *Gauntlet,* circling close around the mast head, cocking their heads to one side as if examining it or peering down on deck, always on the watch for any scrap of food astern.

One o'clock Sunday morning a light appeared off the starboard bow and the captain's hopes were raised by the sight. The navigator was called out to have a look, but after watching it awhile they noticed it moved along the horizon, which meant it was some steamer's mast-head light, evidently a ship coming from Bermuda, bound north.

She passed them about four miles off, but was a most welcome sight, even at that distance, as it was the first vessel seen in six days. The gray dawn, turning to yellow and gold when the sun appeared on the eastern horizon, replaced the starry canopy overhead with a pure, deep blue sky from horizon to horizon.

The sea was a smooth, sparkling expanse of blue, mirrored from the sky with long, gentle swells rolling across it.

The navigator got a good morning observation and gave the captain some instruction in figuring longitude. The position showed the sloop had made ninety-five miles since the day before and left but seventy-five miles more to go.

Early Monday morning all hands were anxiously scanning the western horizon for land.

Bermuda should bear twenty-five miles due south-west of them if the navigator's reckoning was right. His latitude, based on the moon observation, he was sure of, but the longtitude depended on the correctness of his watch, every four seconds variation meaning an error of one mile at sea. *Gauntlet* carried no chronometer, as the other boats did, but depended on the navigator's watch, which he had rated before sailing and of which he felt very confident.

About nine o'clock a bark was discovered hull down to the southward, sailing, as they supposed to the States, until some thoughtful person remarked, "Maybe she's bound for Bermuda."

This increased the excitement of making a land fall.

Close hauled, *Gauntlet* was rapidly overhauling the bark, which they made out later to be a whaler bound for Bermuda. Shortly after noon it grew so black to windward that the halliards were slacked in anticipation of a bad squall. A conical shaped cloud swept down on them. But, though the peak was dropped, it did nothing but rain. For an hour shower after shower came down, killing the light wind.

The bark, between the showers, could clearly be seen three miles away becalmed like *Gauntlet* and rolling on the long southerly swells.

While it rained all hands stayed below, eating the famous repast of the cook's concoction, and, except for the expectation of sighting land, would have been content to stay below.

After the rain a fair northwest wind came in, and with mainsail broad off, the balloon jib was set, but for some time little headway was made against the hard sea.

The breeze gradually increased, as the sky cleared, until *Gauntlet* was sweeping along at a glorious pace.

Something ahead caught the owner's eye and getting on top of the cabin he called for the glasses. One look was enough; there was the light house dead ahead with the island in plain view, not more than ten miles away.

Mr. Hayward, on lookout in the lighthouse, sighted *Gauntlet* at the same time, and telephoned the people in the island that she was in sight. An hour later people in New York got the news by cable message.

The heavy, clumsy bark was left far astern; her heavy sails would not stay filled, but kept slatting the wind out every roll, while the balloon jib on *Gauntlet* pulled like a team of oxen.

"THE HEAVY, CLUMSY BARK WAS LEFT FAR ASTERN".

The stake boat, which was to be anchored two miles off the light, was just steaming out to its position, so *Gauntlet* laid a course to cross close to her stern.

Declining the services of a darky pilot as they swept past their long whale boat, the pilot informed them, "The other boat finished yesterday."

199

This set them guessing. The pilot had said *boat,* not boats. Could it be possible they were second?

This was the question on all lips as *Gauntlet* swept across the finish line and were told the *Tamerlane* had beaten them five hours on time allowance. This made them second boat at any rate and as it proved later the only two to finish, for the big yawl *Lila,* having been dismasted, put into Hampton Roads.

Nearing the island the *Gauntlet* was met by a little knockabout with a friend of the skipper, Stanley McCallan, in it. Laying up in the wind he came aboard to pump handle the arms of her crew and offer congratulations to the nervy little woman.

A HERALD tug took them in tow to the quarantine station, where the doctor came aboard and gave a clear bill of health.

While *Gauntlet* lay off quarantine waiting for the doctor the club steamer came alongside with a great many members on board. They gave three hearty cheers for the *Gauntlet,* followed by three cheers for Mrs. Robinson. To achieve a difficult feat is a satisfaction in itself; to receive congratulations for having done it is pleasant, but those who do accomplish a thing as a rule would rather hide than be held up to the gaze of the multitude.

But there was no dodging the hospitality and congratulations when such people as Dr. and Mrs. Prot, Messrs. Gilbert, Butterfield; Masters Darrell, Pitt, Tucker, Gray, and Gosling came alongside.

A twelve-mile tow brought them to Hamilton Harbor, where *Gauntlet* was tied up to a government buoy amid the cheers of hundreds of spectators on shore and in the small boats that flocked about her. *Tamerlane* saluted her consort with twenty-one guns, and Mrs. Robinson gracefully accepted a bouquet of flowers from admirers in a row boat.

A keeper was put aboard the little sloop, while female friends took the mate ashore to supper and drove her in a carriage to friends in St. George's, with whom she stayed while the yacht was at Bermuda. At the club house, after a hearty dinner and bath, three happy men turned in to sleep as civilized folk once more, too tired to dream or care for squalls.

This interesting account of the first Bermuda race
was published in the March 1907 issue of
the magazine FORE 'N 'AFT. It is reprinted with the
kind permission of Mr. Northam Warren, a former editor of FORE 'N 'AFT.

Cape Cod cat

Designed by Charles D. Mower

A NUMBER of readers, a surprisingly large number in fact, have written and asked for plans of a *genuine* catboat. A cat of the type made famous years ago on the Cape and used on a great many bodies of water from Maine to Florida, a beamy cat of ample proportions for day sailing and overnight cruises, a simply rigged cat of practical nature, in all a well designed catboat of reliable nature.

In going through our collection of plans of small boats here at Anchordown, we came across a smart little catboat designed by the late Mr. Charles D. Mower, who undoubtedly was the most versatile designer of small racing and cruising boats of his time. Mr. Mower left the drawings of this 20 footer with my father a great many years ago as an example of a typical catboat.

My father recalls that Mr. Mower was enthusiastic about catboats and the cat rig, having during the era of the Sonder class, rigged one of these racing machines with a tall, narrow, catboat sail plan. The catboat, he felt, had a definite place in the world of small boats and was a type which he recommended. Despite the fact that the knockabout rigged one-design has grown tremendously in popularity, thus placing the cat among the ranks of old fashioned craft, the single sail of the catboat is still very much in evidence on Barnegat Bay, the Great South Bay at Marblehead and other Down East waters, and various other yachting centers.

The simplicity of the cat rig is a recommendation in itself. There is only one sail and one sheet to handle and the advantages of this feature, particularly when sailing alone, are many. The straight stem, with no bowsprit, is a great convenience in making landings and coming up to floats or docks. The hull possesses many excellent characteristics, not least of which is the great beam which makes the boat able to stand up and carry her sail, provides room for a large cockpit and is the source of the comfort of a boat which does not heel excessively.

This particular catboat does not have a rig as great in area as many, but it is one that will not require reefing very often, and with it she will be a smart sailer. The little boat surely has an attractive out-

201

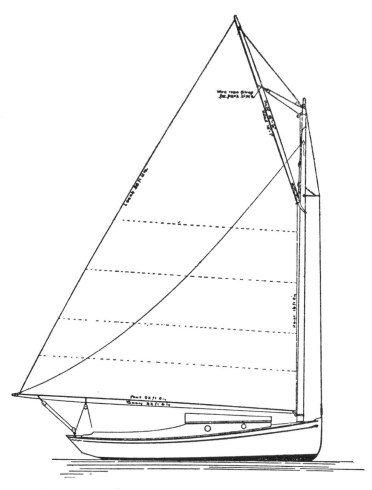

A BOAT OF YESTERDAY?—NOT NECESSARILY—THE CAT RIG IS MAIN-
TAINING ITS POPULARITY. AND FOR ABILITY?—RECENTLY *Tabby*, AN
18 FT. CAT, OWNED BY MR. JOHN KILLAM MURPHY OF BRANFORD,
CONN., WON SEVERAL FIRSTS IN IMPORTANT RACING EVENTS. AS FOR
COMFORT AND EASY SAILING NOTHING CAN COMPARE WITH THE SINGLE
SAIL OF THE CAT RIG. AND FOR SHEER RACING PLEASURE A CATBOAT IS
DIFFICULT TO BEAT. MR. MOWER'S DESIGN, REPRODUCED ABOVE, IS TYP-
ICALLY CAT—A BOAT OF YESTERDAY, TODAY AND TOMORROW.

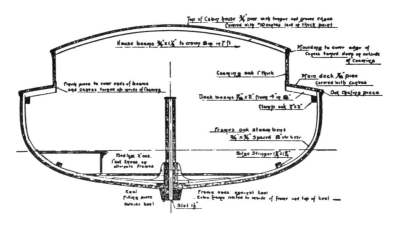

CONSTRUCTION SECTION OF THE 20 FT. CATBOAT DESIGNED BY
THE LATE MR. CHARLES D. MOWER.

board profile, and is simplicity itself. A single stay, leading from the
stem head, over a short jumper, to the masthead comprises her standing
rigging.

The arrangement consists of a stowage space in the eyes of the
boat, abaft which, either side, are two berths. I imagine the cushions of
these berths were covered with a fine grade of soft, dark green corduroy,
quilted with many little tufts. A galley, athwartships at the after end
of the cabin on the port hand and a clothes locker to starboard, with the
companionway between these, completes the interior arrangement. The
large self-bailing cockpit provides grand room for day sailing. There
are many different *types* of catboats of varying hull form, but all with
the single sail. The Shrewsbury River type, for example, was even
more beamy in comparison to length, than the one shown here and
had entirely different sections. In passing—a very old Shrewsbury River
cat was a winter neighbor of the aluminum lady of the New Look,
mentioned in STRONG RIPPLES up in the for'd part of this book. We've
roughly estimated the age of this catboat at somewhere around 60 to
70 years. Her sections show a much flatter form than Mr. Mower's design. There is a slight reverse turn at the keel in all of her sections with
a great deal more deadrise. Her hull form is like that of an old New
York Bay sandbagger of about 1880. The stem of the Shrewsbury cat
has a decided rake aft and the tumble home in the topsides continues

203

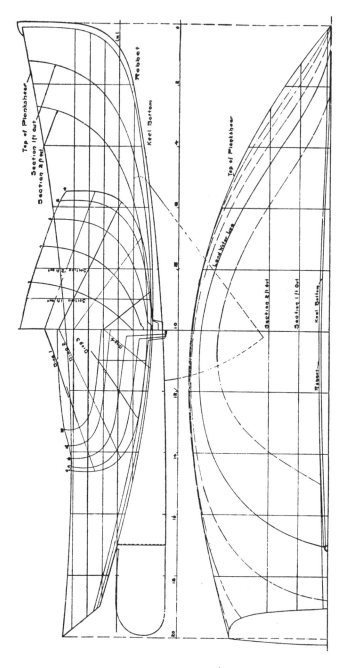

THIS MOWER CAT WAS DEVELOPED AFTER THE TYPE BUILT BY MR. C. C. HANLEY IN THE EARLY NINETEEN HUNDREDS. THERE ARE MANY VARIATIONS OF THE CATBOAT HULL FORM, THO MOST WERE PRODUCED ON, OR NEAR, THE CAPE. FOR EXAMPLE, MR. HORACE S. CROSBY'S MODELS OF 1870 WERE STRAIGHT SECTIONED WITH A GREAT DEAL MORE DEADRISE THAN THE HANLEY (OR MOWER) CAT.

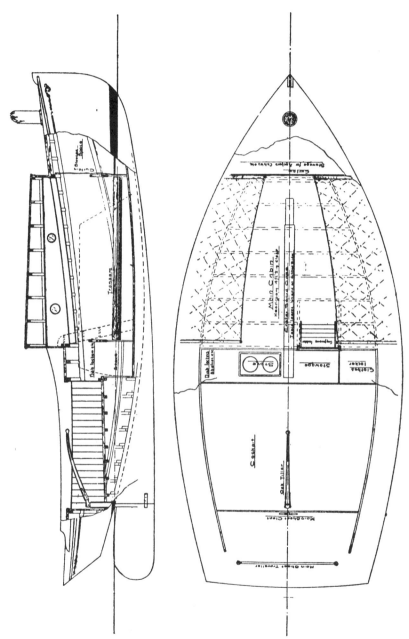

ARRANGEMENT PLAN OF THE 20 FT. MOWER CAT.

205

the entire length of the boat. So you can easily see, upon examining the lines of the Mower catboat, how entirely different these two "catboats" are—and there are other variations as well in boats of this kind.

It is indeed an interesting and absorbing subject, this "development" of hull forms in various localities—and the catboat is but one of the many boats in which such variations exist, for the sharpie of New Haven, the skipjack of the Chesapeake, the sloops of Friendship fame, the sampan of the Orient, the skiffs of the New Jersey coast; are all individual developments over a period of hundreds of years. Each has its own characteristics and purpose for different localities. Surprisingly enough, though these hull forms were developed years and years before the days of any kind of rapid, or even slow, communication and at places many miles apart, there is an amazing similarity in the "local" types built the world over. But that is a subject in itself, and will be covered in some future issue of our series of books which has been conceived to promote and create further interest in wholesome little boats of all kinds.

Mr. James S. Pitkin, of DUFFLEBAG fame, and a writer of authoritative articles on the subject of yachts and yachting, purchased a catboat early last year. In connection with this he has written, ". . . I have been most frightfully busy sailing my ideal catboat—and when I say 'ideal' I mean it absolutely! I found her on Buzzards Bay—a genuine Crosby that had been in storage for some years in a private boathouse on a gentleman's estate . . . she is 21 ft. over all with a 9 ft. 6 in. beam. Her cabin has two large berths, toilet, galley, etcetera. And with her mahogany trim she is a very pretty boat—very pretty indeed.

"The only thing wrong with her was her sail. This was cut in the usual way—long on the foot, short on the hoist and flat on the head—the sort of sail that has given the catboat the stigma of being hard on the helm. Of course, she had a wheel—a silly affectation on a 21 ft. boat.

"I designed a new sail shorter on the foot, longer on the hoist and peaked up sufficiently to bring the center of effort where it belonged . . . I had the wheel replaced by a tiller—I derived no pleasure from steering with a wheel as it has no 'feel'. Also, I shifted the lead ballast. Now she will sail herself, in a moderate breeze at sea. At no time does she take a helm that a boy of ten could not handle easily. And she handles like a knockabout. And she is fast. At all events, she sailed from Cape Cod Canal to Branford—120 miles—in fourteen hours flat.

This, I regard as fast going for a boat of her size and type. To be sure, the conditions were favorable—a fresh off-shore breeze, a bit abaft the beam, that held steady hour after hour.

"I named her *Sally* after Sally Crosby who was known as 'the prettiest girl on Cape Cod.' She was a great aunt of the boat's builder and married Captain Jeremiah Mayo, who became master of a brig at the age of twenty-two, engaged in trans-Atlantic trade. He named his vessel after his pretty wife. When he was at Havre, after Waterloo, friends of the Emperor asked Captain Mayo if he would take Napoleon to America.

"Thinking", wrote Captain Mayo in his journal, "how surprised Sally would be, I agreed immediately."

"As it happened, the British intervened, and Napoleon set sail for Saint Helena, instead of Cape Cod.

"The young captain's desire to surprise his bride by having Napoleon Bonaparte come strolling up the garden path of the little cottage at Brewster, on Cape Cod, has always appealed to me. So I welcomed the opportunity to pay my respects to Sally and her gallant Captain."

All of which goes to prove the sincere admiration and devotion Mr. Pitkin has for his little catboat.

Mr. Mower's catboat, to again return to our description, is 20 ft. 0 in. over all and 16 ft. 4 in. on her designed water line. She has an extreme breadth of 9 ft. 3 in. and is 8 ft. 3 in. in breadth on her designed waterline. Her draft is 1 ft. 7 in. with the board up.

I feel sure she too has all the loveliness and ideal qualities of little *Sally*. Perhaps you may find this true, someday.

John Atkin.

We're Here

William Atkin

WE OF ANCHORDOWN LOOK FORWARD WITH ANTICIPA-
TION TO THE BUILDING OF A LITTLE BOAT FOR OUR
OWN USE — A SIMPLE POWER BOAT CARRYING A STEADY-
ING SAIL AND AN ENGINE OF VERY MODEST POWER ⇥
THE LINES HAVE BEEN LAID DOWN FULL SIZE, HALF THE FRA-
MES ARE MADE, AND THE KEEL IS SAWN TO SHAPE BUT IT
NEEDS PUTTING TOGETHER ⇥ ALL THE REQUIRED LUM-
BER IS IN HAND AND SEASONED, AND MUCH OF THE HARD-
WARE, EQUIPMENT, FASTENINGS, AND MISCELLANEOUS
GEAR WAITS TO BE USED ⇥ THE ENGINE STANDS READY
IN THE GARAGE AND THE SHAFTING, PROPELLER AND STUFF-
ING BOX ARE ON THE WAY ⇥ ⇥ ⇥ ⇥

THE POWER BOAT WE ARE LOOKING FORWARD TO LAUNCHING ONE
OF THESE FINE DAYS WE EXPECT TO NAME *WE'RE HERE*, AND
WHAT MANNER OF CRAFT SHE WILL BE IS ILLUSTRATED BY
THE PLANS WHICH GRACE THESE PAGES ⇥ ⇥ ⇥

BEFORE SETTING UP THE KEEL WE SHALL HAVE TO LENGTHEN THE
DINGHY SHED, THE COZY WORK SHOP WHICH STANDS
IN THE REAR OF ANCHOR DOWN ⇥ ⇥ ⇥

THIS, HOWEVER,
IS NOT A
LARGE UNDER-
TAKING ⇥ I
HAVE WRITTEN
MANY TIMES
THAT THE BEST

↳ THE LENGTHENED DINGHY SHED ⇥

WAY TO GET A BOAT IS TO BUILD IT ONESELF — AND THIS
IS WHAT WE ARE DOING ⇥ ONE ADVANTAGE OF THIS

208

UNDER WAY WITH THE LATHROP ENGINE
HOOKED UP". →

WE'RE HERE

20 FT. WATER LINE POWER BOAT

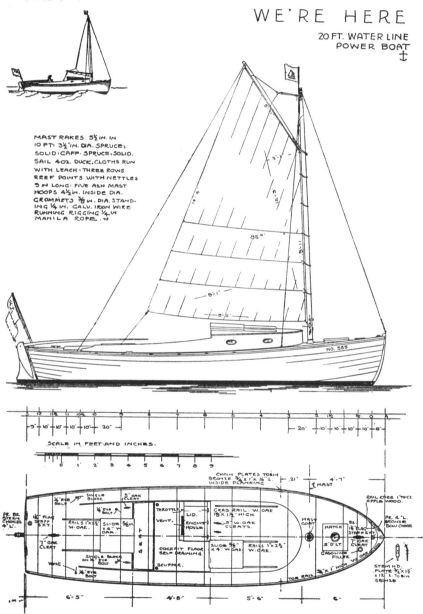

MAST RAKES 5½ IN. IN
10 FT. 3½ IN. DIA. SPRUCE;
SOLID·GAFF·SPRUCE·SOLID.
SAIL 4 OZ. DUCK, CLOTHS RUN
WITH LEACH·THREE ROWS
REEF POINTS WITH NETTLES
9 IN LONG· FIVE ASH MAST
HOOPS 4½ IN. INSIDE DIA.
GROMMETS ⅜ IN. DIA. STAND-
ING ¼ IN. GALV. IRON WIRE
RUNNING RIGGING ¼ IN
MANILA ROPE . →

SCALE IN FEET AND INCHES.

THE COCKPIT FLOOR OF WE'RE HERE STANDS 5 IN. ABOVE THE WATERLINE AND IS SELF DRAINING
THROUGH 1¼ IN. DIA. RUBBER HOSE·EACH SIDE· USE BRONZE FITTINGS AND BRONZE HOSE CLAMPS →

209

IS THAT IF MISTAKES ARE MADE IT IS NOT NECESSARY TO PAY
SOMEONE ELSE FOR MAKING THEM ⇥ AND THERE ARE MANY
OTHER ADVANTAGES I SHALL NOT ENUMERATE ⇥ ⇥ ⇥

THE LINES OF *WE'RE HERE* SHOW A V BOTTOM SEABRIGHT
SKIFF, A DEVISING OF MY OWN ⇥ THE OVERALL LENGTH
IS, 21 FT. 8 IN.; WATERLINE LENGTH, 20 FT.; THE BREADTH,
5 FT. 10 IN.; AND THE DRAFT, 1 FT. 3 IN. ⇥ THE FREEBOARD
AT THE BOW IS, 2 FT. 10 IN.; THE
LEAST FREEBOARD,
1 FT. 9 IN.; WHILE
AT THE STERN IT IS
2 FT. 0 IN. ⇥ THE
STRAIGHT FLAT
KEEL IN THIS
PARTICULAR
DESIGN IS

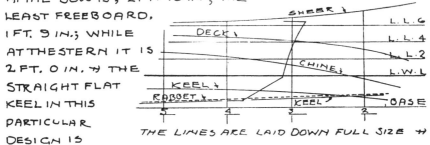

THE LINES ARE LAID DOWN FULL SIZE ⇥

MUCH LESS IN BREADTH THAN IN MY OLDER DESIGNS OF
BOATS OF THIS CHARACTER ⇥ *WE'RE HERE* IS A NARROW
CRAFT COMPARED TO PRESENT TRENDS AND I DO NOT BE-
LIEVE ANYONE WILL BE JUSTIFIED IN SAYING SHE IS A "CUT-
OFF BOX" ⇥ THERE IS A LOT TO BE SAID FOR THE SEA-
BRIGHT SKIFF MODEL; NOT LEAST OF WHICH IS THAT THIS
FORM IS EXCELLENT IN ROUGH WATER AND FAST WITH MOD-
ERATE POWER ⇥ ⇥ ⇥

ANOTHER FEATURE ABOUT THE SEABRIGHT SKIFF HULL-FORM
IS THE EASE WITH WHICH IT CAN BE HANDLED ASHORE ⇥ A
MARINE RAILWAY OR SPECIAL CRADLE IS NOT REQUIRED
FOR HAULING OUT; FOUR PLANKS, A TACKLE FALL AND
THREE ROLLERS ARE NEEDED — A SHELVING SHORE — AND NOTH-
ING MORE ⇥ FOR WINTER STORAGE WE SHALL USE THE GAR-
DEN LAWN; THUS AVOIDING THE DELAYS AND EXASPERATIONS
OF OVER-CROWDED BOAT STORAGE YARDS, TO SAY NOTHING OF
THE EXPENSE ATTACHED THERETO ⇥ SINCE *WE'RE HERE*
WILL SIT UPRIGHT WITHOUT DAMAGE ON HER OWN BOTTOM

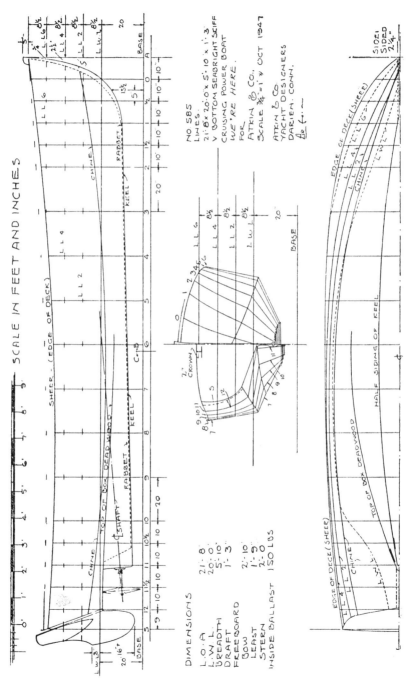

SCALE IN FEET AND INCHES

NO 585
LINES.
21·8 x 20·0 x 5·10 x 1·3
V BOTTOM SEABRIGHT SKIFF
CRUISING POWER BOAT
WE'RE HERE.
FOR
ATKIN & CO.
SCALE ¾" = 1'·0 OCT 1947

ATKIN & CO.
YACHT DESIGNERS
DARIEN, CONN.

DIMENSIONS
L.O.A   21·8
L.W.L   20·0·
BREADTH   5·10·
DRAFT   1·3
FREEBOARD
  BOW   2·0·
  LEAST   1·5·
  STERN   1·0·
INSIDE BALLAST   150 LBS

211

THE LITTLE BOAT WILL BE EASY TO TOTE OVERLAND ON A
TRAILER OR SMALL TRUCK ⌁ ⌁ ⌁

BECAUSE THE PLANS ARE UNUSUAL-
LY COMPLETE AND SHOW THE
FORM, MATERIALS, CON-
STRUCTION, ARRANGE-
MENT, ENGINE IN-
STALLATION, AND
RIG OF THE BOAT IT
SEEMS UNECESSARY
TO GO INTO DETAIL CON-
CERNING THESE MATTERS ⌁ ⌁ ⌁

SEABRIGHT SKIFFS AND — A
SHELVING SHORE ⌁

HOWEVER IT MAY BE OF SPECIAL INTEREST TO MENTION
THE REASON FOR SOME OF THE FEATURES OF THE DESIGN;
NOT LEAST OF THESE IS THE WHITE OAK PLANKING ⌁ THE BEST
DAYS FOR CRUISING COME IN THE FALL AND EARLY WINTER⌁
THIN SKIMS OF ICE MAY ALSO COME IN EARLY WINTER ⌁ A
BOAT PLANKED WITH SOFT WOOD WILL BE QUICKLY AND
BADLY DAMAGED IF IT IS PUSHED THRU ICE; OAK PLANKING
WILL STAND A LOT OF ROUGH USAGE UNDER THESE WINTER-
TIME CONDITIONS ⌁   THE TOP-SIDE PLANKING HAS LAPPED
SEAMS; LESS LIKELY TO SHRINK DURING DRY SEASONS ⌁
THE BOTTOM PLANKING IS ½ IN. THICK WHITE OAK, SEAMS
CAULKED; INTERCOSTAL FRAMES WILL PREVENT SEAMS FROM
WEAVING AND THE CAULKING FROM CREEPING ⌁ FASTEN-
INGS THROUGHOUT ARE TOBIN BRONZE BOLTS, EVERDUR SCREWS
AND COPPER RIVETS ⌁   THE DECK, TRUNK CABIN, COAMINGS,
JOINER WORK, AND EVERYTHING ABOVE THE SHEER LINE
WILL BE AS LIGHT AS POSSIBLE ⌁ MOST POWER BOATS ARE
AS LIGHT AS POSSIBLE *BELOW* THE SHEER LINE AND IMPRAC-
TICALLY HEAVY *ABOVE* THIS LINE, WHICH IS ONE OF THE
REASONS MOST POWER BOATS ROLL BADLY ⌁ THE ENGINE
WEIGHT IS LOW IN *WE'RE HERE* AND WE SHALL CARRY
A SUITABLE WEIGHT OF INSIDE LEAD BALLAST ⌁

212

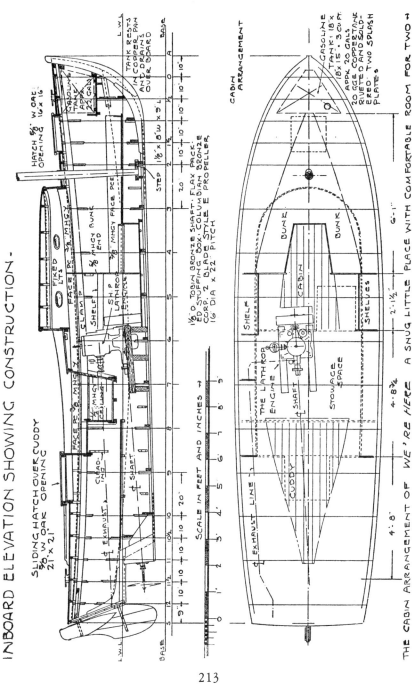

THE COCKPIT IS SOMEWHAT ABAFT AMIDSHIP AND IS SELF-BAILING ≈ THE LITTLE BOAT HAS PROPER DECKS EITHER SIDE THE CABIN TRUNK, COCKPIT AND AFTER HATCH ≈ AND NOTE WELL — A LONG AFTER DECK; NO SWAMPING HER IF A BIG ONE COMES OVER THE STERN, AND NO CHORE PUMPING THE BILGE DRY AFTER EVERY RAIN ≈ THE BILGE IN ALL DECKED BOATS ALWAYS SHOULD BE DRY; THERE IS ONLY ONE REASON FOR A LEAKY BOAT — CARELESS WORKMANSHIP ≈ ≈

THE TRUNK CABIN IS LOW — AND LOOKS LIKE A TRUNK CABIN WITHOUT BENEFIT OF USELESS CURVES, ROUNDINGS, & OTHER AUTOMOBILE PRACTICES ≈ THE AFTER DECK IS PIERCED WITH A SHIP-SHAPE SLIDING HATCH, THE COAMINGS ARE HIGH AND THERE IS AN ESCAPE HATCH IN THE FORWARD DECK WHICH ALSO SERVES AS AN EFFECTIVE VENTILATOR, AND, AS WILL BE SEEN, AN AUXILIARY SAILING RIG ≈ ≈ ≈

WE BORROWED THE DESIGN OF THIS FROM MR. CONOR O'BRIAN, A CRUISING MAN FOR WHOM WE HAVE PROFOUND RESPECT AND ADMIRATION ≈ ROVE FOR BRAILS (NOT SHOWN ON THE SAIL PLAN) SAIL CAN BE TAKEN IN INSTANTLY AND EASILY — AND RESET AS QUICKLY ≈ WE'RE HERE, BECAUSE OF THE VERY SHALLOW DRAFT, WILL NOT GO TO WINDWARD UNDER CANVAS, HOWEVER SHE WILL REACH AND RUN ≈ THE SAIL WILL, BY THE WAY, BE PROPERLY TANNED AND THUS WILL NOT REQUIRE DRYING AFTER EVERY WETTING ≈ ≈ ≈

FOR WINDWARD WORK WE SHALL DEPEND UPON THE ENGINE ≈ THIS IS A 5 H.P. SINGLE CYLINDER TWO CYCLE LATHROP WEIGHING 325 LBS. ≈ IT WAS BUILT NEARLY A QUARTER CENTURY AGO BY THE LATHROP ENGINE COMPANY, MYSTIC, CONN. AND IS DESIGNED TO DEVELOP POWER AT LOW REVOLUTIONS ≈ WE PURCHASED THE ENGINE FROM A MAN AT BRANFORD, CONN. WHO HAD USED IT IN A SMALL WORK BOAT FOR 12 YEARS ≈ I UNDERSTAND HE WAS THE SECOND OWNER ≈ THE PROPELLER THE FORMER OWNER USED

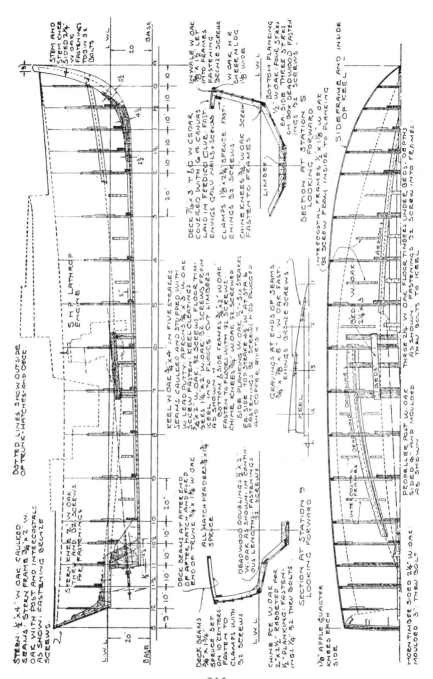

WITH THE ENGINE WAS A THREE BLADE WIDE BLADE TYPE 17 IN. DIA. BY 22 IN. PITCH COLUMBIAN ~ ITSPUN THIS AT 600 TURNS A MINUTE, SO YOU CAN SEE THIS IS AN ENGINE OF SOMETHING MORE THAN "PEANUT" HORSE POWER ~ ~ ~

THERE WAS A TIME WHEN I FELT I KNEW A GREAT DEAL ABOUT GASOLINE ENGINES, HAVING DESIGNED ONE OF 800 H.P., AND WORKED ON MANY OTHERS; BUT THAT WAS MANY YEARS AGO ~ OTHER THINGS BEING EQUAL, LIGHT RE-CIPROCATING PARTS SPELL INCREASED REVOLUTIONS, GREATER POWER AND LESS VIBRATION ~ WITH THESE THOUGHTS IN MIND WE DECIDED TO FIT THE RELIABLE OLD LATHROP WITH AN ALUMINUM PISTON ~ THE GOOD PEOPLE AT MYSTIC LOANED US THE PATTERNS FROM WHICH THE ORIGINAL PISTON WAS MADE AND FROM THESE WE HAD LIGHT ALLOY CASTINGS MADE ~ THESE WERE ALLOWED TO SEASON FOR SEVERAL MONTHS AND WERE THEN TAKEN TO THE LATHROP PLANT FOR MACHINING ~ NEW RINGS, BRONZE WRIST PIN BUSHINGS AND A HOLLOW WRIST PIN WERE FITTED TO ONE OF THE LIGHT PISTONS AND THE OTHER KEPT AS A SPARE ~ THE ALUMINUM PISTON WEIGHED APPROXIMATELY ONE THIRD AS MUCH AS THE IRON ONE ~ WE FEEL WHEN NEXT WE SWING THE FLYWHEEL AGAINST THE COMPRESSION "OLD RELIABLE" WILL SPIN AROUND AT BETWEEN 725 AND 750 TURNS PER MINUTE AND EASILY TURN A 16 IN. DIA. BY 22 IN. PITCH TWO BLADE STYLE "E" COLUMBIAN PROPELLER ~ ~ ~

SOMETHING MORE THAN "PEANUT" HORSE POWER ~

IN THESE DAYS OF QUANITY PRODUCTION WE FOUND IT SOME-THING OF A FRAGRANT NOVELTY TO VISIT AND HAVE WORK DONE AT THE LATHROP FACTORY; THE WORK IN HAND WAS BEAUTIFULLY DONE WITH ACCURACY, EFFICIENCY AND

216

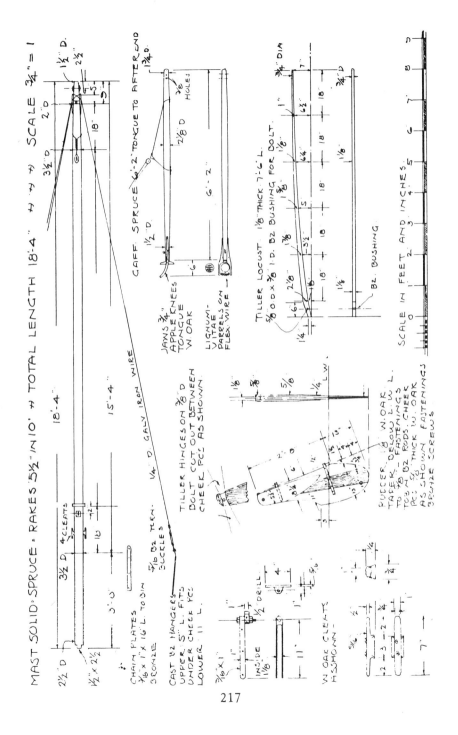

MAST SOLID SPRUCE • RAKES 5½" IN 10' • TOTAL LENGTH 18'-4"   " " "   SCALE ¾" = 1

GAFF SPRUCE 6'-2" TONGUE TO AFTER END

TILLER LOCUST 1⅛" THICK 7'-6" L.
⅝" O D × ⅜" I. D. BZ BUSHING FOR BOLT.

SCALE IN FEET AND INCHES

217

DISPATCH ⅋ AND HOW REFRESHING TO SEE THE INTEREST THIS
HALF CENTURY OLD CONCERN HAS IN ITS OLD MODELS — WHICH,
BY THE WAY, NEVER BECOME OBSOLETE ⅋ ⅋ ⅋

MY OLD FRIEND, MR. FLOYD WEBB, FERRY ROAD, SAYBROOK,
CONN., TOOK DOWN THE ENGINE AND GAVE IT A COMPLETE OVER-
HAUL ; ITS *FIRST!* ⅋ THERE WAS PLENTY OF GREASE AND
RUST OUTSIDE BUT ALL WAS WELL INSIDE AND LITTLE SIGN OF
WEAR ⅋ SO THIS INGENIOUS AND VERY EXPERT MECHANI-
CIAN CLEANED OFF THE RUST AND GREASE, REFITTED,
SCRAPED, POLISHED AND BURNISHED THE BRONZE, STEEL AND
IRON PARTS UNTIL THEY WERE NEW, FITTED THE ALUMINUM
PISTON, AND REPAINTED THE HUSKY OLD LADY IN A DRESS OF
GRAY ⅋ THE ONLY NEW PARTS NEEDED WERE : SPARK PLUG,
STARTING PIN, IGNITER SPRINGS, EXHAUST FLANGE ⅋ ⅋ ⅋

ONE MORE FEATURE ABOUT *WE'RE HERE* ⅋ THE ENGINE IS SET
OFF CENTER AND THE SHAFT SPLAYS TO STARBOARD, THE
PROPELLER TURNS TO THE RIGHT HAND AND IS ON THE CEN-
TER OF THE BOX DEADWOOD ⅋ THE PURPOSE OF THIS IS TO
BALANCE THE SIDE THRUST OF THE PROPELLER BY THE
OBLIQUE THRUST OF THE PROPELLER STREAM ⅋ WITH THIS
ARRANGEMENT THE LITTLE BOAT WILL STEER EASILY AND
FOLLOW A STRAIGHT COURSE WITHOUT THE AID OF THE RUD-
DER, A CHARACTERISTIC VERY FEW POWER BOATS HAVE ⅋ ⅋ ⅋

IF MY EXPERIENCE IN THE PAST AND CALCULATIONS IN THE
PRESENT ARE A RELIABLE BASIS FROM WHICH TO WORK, OUR
MODIFIED SEABRIGHT SKIFF CRUISING POWER BOAT WILL HAVE
A SPEED OF 12 MILES AN HOUR, THANKS TO ITS ADVANCED DE-
SIGN AND THE URGE OF THE LATHROP ENGINE ⅋ ⅋ ⅋

SO, SHIPMATES, THUS ENDS ⅋ ⅋ ⅋

TYPOGRAPHY AFTER THE MANNER OF
M. MAURICE C DAUWAERT, EDITOR, WANDELAER ET SUR L'EAU.

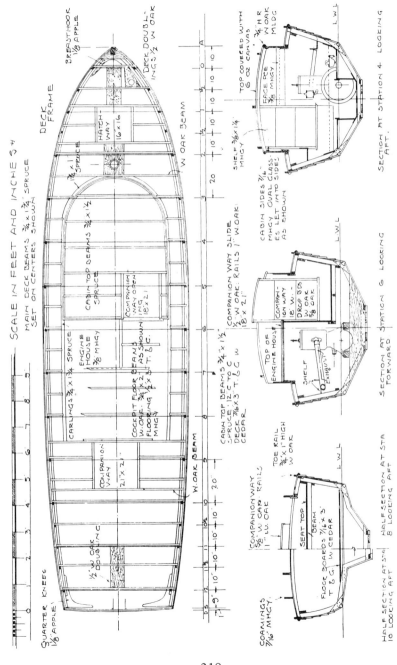

ATHWARTSHIP SECTIONS SHOWING LOCATION OF BUNKS · ENGINE · COMPANION WAY · FLOOR BOARDS WE'RE HERE.

HALF SECTION AT STA 10 LOOKING AFT

HALF SECTION AT STA 8 LOOKING AFT

SECTION AT STATION 6 LOOKING FORWARD

SECTION AT STATION 4 LOOKING AFT

219